RS

BOB SHAW

THE TWO-TIMERS

UNABRIDGED

PAN BOOKS LTD : LONDON

First published in Great Britain 1969 by Victor Gollancz Ltd.
This edition published 1971 by Pan Books Ltd,
33 Tothill Street, London, S.W.1

ISBN 0 330 02671 2

Printed and bound in England by
Hazell Watson & Viney Ltd,
Aylesbury, Bucks

ONE

TO BRETON–TRAPPED in his nexus of boredom – the sound of the telephone was almost beautiful. He got to his feet and walked across the living-room towards the hall.

'Who would that be, darling?' Kate Breton frowned slightly as she spoke, annoyed at the interruption.

Breton ran a mental eye over the quiver full of sarcasms which immediately offered itself, and finally – in deference to their guests – selected one of the least lethal.

'I don't quite recognize the ring,' he said evenly, noting the sudden faint compression of Kate's chalk-pink lips. She would remember that one, for discussion, probably at 3.00 AM when he was trying to sleep.

'Good old John – still sharp as a razor.' Gordon Palfrey spoke quickly, in his stand-back-and-let-me-be-tactful voice, and Miriam Palfrey smiled her bland Aztec smile beneath eyes like nail heads. The Palfreys were two of his wife's latest acquisitions and their presence in Breton's home usually caused a fretful, burning pain in his stomach. Smiling numbly, he closed the living-room door behind him and picked up the phone.

'Hello,' he said. 'John Breton speaking.'

'We're calling ourselves John now, are we? It used to be Jack.' The male voice on the wire had a tense, controlled quality about it, as though the speaker was suppressing a strong emotion – fear, perhaps, or triumph.

'Who is this?' Breton tried unsuccessfully to identify the voice, uneasily aware that the phone line was a portal through which anybody anywhere could project himself right into his house. When he opened the channel to alien ideas he was placing himself at a disadvantage unless the caller announced his name, and the idea seemed completely unfair. 'Who is this speaking?'

'So you really don't know. That's inter-*esting*.'

Something about the words gave Breton a vague thrill of alarm. 'Look,' he said tersely. 'Either state your business or hang up.'

'Don't get angry, John – I'll be happy to do both those things. I called simply to make sure you and Kate were at home before I came over there. And now I'll hang up.'

'Hold on for just one moment,' Breton snapped, aware that he was letting the unknown caller get too far under his skin. 'You haven't said what you think you're going to get.'

'My wife, of course,' the voice replied pleasantly. 'You've been living with my wife for almost exactly nine years – and I'm coming to take her back.'

The phone clicked and began to purr blandly in Breton's ear. He tapped the rest button several times before realizing he was acting out a visual cliché implanted in his mind by old movies – once a caller has broken the connexion, jiggling the rest never brings him back. Swearing under his breath, Breton put the phone down and stood beside it undecidedly for several seconds.

The whole thing must be a devious hoax, but who was behind it?

He knew only one confirmed practical joker – Carl Tougher, the geologist in Breton's engineering consultancy. But when he had last seen Tougher, in the office that afternoon, the geologist had been grimly trying to sort out a snarl-up in a survey the company had undertaken for the siting of a cement works over by Silverstream. Breton had never seen him look more worried, and less like playing games, especially one so full of uneasy subtleties. This conversation had been meaningless – which was not too surprising considering the mentality of phone cranks – but there had been uncomfortable undertones in it as well. For he no longer called himself Jack. Breton had begun using the formal version of his name for image reasons at the time his business began to develop, but that had been years ago and – he felt a surge of indignation – it was nobody's concern but his own. All the same, some stubborn corner of his mind had never approved of the name change, and it was almost as if the unknown caller had been able to see right through him and pinpoint the tiny shadow that was his tumour of guilt.

Breton paused at the living-room door, realizing he was reacting just the way the phone crank would have wanted – turning the thing over and over in his mind instead of dismissing it. He glanced around the orange-lit panelling of the hall, suddenly wishing he had moved to a bigger and newer place last year as Kate had wanted. He had outgrown his old house, and should have discarded it without sentiment long ago. *You have been living with my wife for almost exactly nine years*. Breton frowned as he remembered the words – the caller had not been implying he had an earlier marriage to Kate, or anything like that, because she and Breton had been married eleven years. But that figure of nine years seemed to mean something, to have multi-layered connexions of anxiety, as though some part of his subconscious had drunk in its significance and was awaiting apprehensively for the next move.

'For God's sake!' Breton spoke aloud and smacked his forehead in self-disgust. 'I'm nearly as crazy as he is.'

He opened the door and went into the living-room. In his absence Kate had dimmed the lights and moved a coffee table over beside Miriam Palfrey. A block of plain white paper and a pen were ready on the table, and Miriam's stubby, grub-like fingers were already making vague little floating movements over them. Breton groaned silently – so they were going to have a session after all. The Palfreys were newly back from a three-month tour of Europe and all evening had been so full of the trip that he had begun to think there would be no demonstration. The hope had given him the strength to listen politely to their tourist talk.

'Who was on the phone, darling?'

'I don't know.' Breton did not want to talk about the call.

'Wrong number?'

'Yes.'

Kate's eyes searched his face. 'But you were there so *long*. And I thought I heard you shouting.'

'Well,' Breton said impatiently, 'let's say it was the right number, but the wrong people.'

Gordon Palfrey snorted delightedly and the light of interest in Kate's eyes dwindled away into disappointed coldness, as if Breton had switched off two minute television sets. That was another one for the nightly post mortem in the small hours, when all normal people were asleep and even the curtains of their rooms were breathing steadily in the night breezes. Why, he wondered guiltily, do I hurt Kate in the presence of her friends? But then, why does she hurt me all the time – showing her damned determined indifference to the business, year in and year out, but giving me a public third degree about a stupid telephone call? He sat down heavily, let his right hand instinctively guide itself to his whisky glass, and glanced around the room, practising his benign smile on the Palfreys.

Gordon Palfrey was toying with the square of black velvet, figured with silver stars, which was always draped over his wife's face during the sessions – but he still wanted to go on talking about Europe. He launched into a long account, undeterred by the theatrical flinches Breton gave each time he heard a statement like 'The French have an excellent colour sense'. His theme was that the décor of European cottages was invariably in better taste than the work of the best American decorators. Sinking back into the amber prison of boredom, Breton writhed in his armchair, wondering how he would survive the evening, knowing he should have been in the office helping Carl Tougher to straighten out the cement plant survey. With the effortless and imperceptible change of gear that is the mark of the born bore, Palfrey slid on to the subject of an old crofter they had met in Scotland who hand-wove tartans in spite of being totally blind, but Miriam had begun to get into her pre-trance restlessness.

'What are you talking about, Gordon?' Miriam Palfrey leaned far back in her chair and her right hand, poised over the block of paper, began to dip and sway like a kite in a high wind.

'I was telling Kate and John about old Hamish.'

'Oh, yes – we enjoyed old Hamish.' Miriam's voice had become a faint monotone which sounded to Breton like an incredibly banal imitation of something from a Bela Lugosi film. Seeing the rapt attention of Kate's face he decided to launch a full-scale attack in defence of common-sense.

'So you enjoyed old Hamish,' he said in an unnaturally loud and cheerful voice. 'What a picture that conjures up! I can see old Hamish slumped in a corner of his croft – an empty, dried-up husk, his purpose in life fulfilled – he has been *enjoyed* by the Palfreys.'

But Kate waved him to silence and Gordon Palfrey, who had been unfolding the velvet square, draped it over Miriam's upturned face. Immediately, her plumply white hand took up the pen and began to fly across the paper, producing line after line of neat script. Gordon knelt beside the coffee table to steady the writing pad and Kate removed each top sheet as it was filled, handling them with a reverence that Breton found more annoying than any other aspect of the whole business. If his wife wanted to take an interest in so-called automatic writing, why could she not have been more rational about it? He would almost have been prepared to help her investigate the phenomenon himself had she not insisted on putting every sample in the general category of a Message From the Other Side.

'Anybody ready for another drinkie?' Breton stood up and walked to the mirror-backed cocktail cabinet. Drinkie, he thought. *Christ! What are they doing to me?* He poured himself a generous shot of Scotch, tempered it with soda, and leaned against the cabinet, watching the tableau at the other side of the room. Miriam Palfrey's body was limp in the chair but her hand was moving as quickly as it was possible to write without the aid of shorthand, producing thirty or more words a minute. The material she turned out was usually flowery, outdated prose on unrelated subjects, with a high proportion of words like Beauty and Love, always written with the initial capital. The Palfreys claimed it was dictated by the spirits of dead authors, whom they tentatively identified on a stylistic basis. Breton had his own ideas, and he had been more shocked than he cared to admit by Kate's uncritical acceptance of what he regarded as a party trick straight out of a Victorian drawing-room.

Sipping steadily at his drink, Breton watched Kate as she gathered up the sheets, numbered the corners and set them in a neat pile. Eleven years of marriage had not made any real physical changes in her – tall and still slim, she wore richly coloured silks as though they were natural plumage, reminding Breton of a gorgeous and exotic bird; but her eyes had grown much older. Suburban neurosis, he thought, that must be it. Fragmentation of the family reflected in the individual. Give it a label and forget it. A woman is never completely a wife until all her own family are dead. Amalgamate orphanages and marriage bureaus. I'm drinking too much . . .

A low gasp of excitement from Kate brought his attention back to the group at the table. Miriam Palfrey's hand had begun to trace what, at that distance, looked like an intricate circular pattern, like a drawing of a freshly opened carnation. He went closer and saw that she was writing in a tight, slowly spreading spiral, moaning faintly and shuddering as the pattern grew. An edge of the black cloth across her upturned face alternately clung and fluttered, like the breathing apparatus of a marine animal.

'What is it?' Breton asked the question reluctantly, not wishing to show too much interest, but aware that this was something new to the writing sessions. Miriam sat up uncertainly as he spoke, and Gordon Palfrey put an arm around her shoulders.

'I don't know,' Kate said, rotating the sheet in her long-fingered hands. 'This is . . . it's a *poem*.'

'Well, let's hear it.' Breton spoke with a tolerant joviality, annoyed at letting himself be sucked in, yet impressed by the sheer manual dexterity Miriam had shown.

Kate cleared her throat and read:

'I have wished for you a thousand nights,
While the green-glow hour-hand slowly veers.
I could weep for the very need of you,
But you wouldn't taste my tears.'

Breton found the lines vaguely disturbing, for no reason he could name. He went back to the cocktail cabinet and, while the others examined the fragment of poetry, stood frowning down into the mirrored array of bottles and glasses. Sipping the tingling ice-warmth of his drink, he stared back at his own eyes in the crystal microcosm; then – quite suddenly – his mind plumbed the possible significance of the phrase 'almost exactly nine years'. That was the real kicker in the call he had received, if he guessed right; it was a psychological depth charge, perfectly aimed, fused to sink deep.

It had been nine years earlier, to the month, that a police cruiser had found Kate wandering in the darkness of 50th Avenue, with flecks of human brain tissue spattered across her face ...

Breton stiffened with shock as the phone shrilled in the hall. He set his glass down with a sharp double click, left the room and picked up the phone.

'Breton here,' he snapped. 'Who's that?'

'Hello, John. What's the matter?' This time the voice was immediately identifiable as that of Carl Tougher.

'Carl!' Breton sank on to a chair, and groped for his cigarettes. 'Did you call me earlier? Within the last half hour?'

'No – I've been too busy.'

'You're sure?'

'What is this, John? I told you I've been too busy – we're in serious trouble over the Silverstream survey.'

'It doesn't check out?'

'That's right. I made a series of eight random readings in our designated area this morning, and checked with a different gravimeter after lunch. As far as I can tell at this point the initial survey we made last month is completely haywire. The new readings are roughly twenty milligals down on what they should be.'

'Twenty! But that would suggest a much lighter rock formation than we thought. It could mean something like—'

'Salt,' Tougher cut in. 'Could you interest the client in a salt mine in place of a cement works?'

Breton put a cigarette into his mouth and lit it, wondering

why the world had chosen this particular evening to begin drifting out of focus. 'Listen, Carl. We can make two interpretations of these discrepancies. The first is the one you've already mentioned – that the limestone we *know* to lie under that site has changed overnight into salt – and, with your support, I'm ruling that one out right now. The other is that somehow both our gravimeters are out of adjustment – right?'

'I guess so,' Tougher said wearily.

'So we rent a couple of new instruments tomorrow and go over the ground again.'

'I thought you'd say that. Do you know how many miles I covered today, John? I feel like I've walked clear across the state of Montana.'

'I'll go with you next time,' Breton replied. 'I need the exercise. See you in the morning, Carl.'

'Yeah, see you. Oh, John – you left out the third possible explanation.'

'Which is? . . .'

'That the force of gravity has lessened since yesterday.'

'Get some rest, Carl – even your jokes are getting tired.' Breton set the phone down and smiled in appreciation of the way in which the little geologist never got depressed or rattled. A telephone crank who picked on Tougher would have ricocheted off a massive shield of sane practicability – yet in this case Tougher was the only suspect Breton had had. His jokes were usually on the locker room level, but there was the time a couple of years earlier when Tougher had spent something like fifteen dollars of his own money in bringing a can of petrol to work every day and sneaking it into the office janitor's car. Later Tougher had explained, matter-of-factly, that he had wanted to study the janitor's reactions when he discovered his car was apparently manufacturing gas instead of using it up. Was that particular hoax on a par with '*You have been living with my wife for almost exactly nine years*'? Breton was uncertain. He went back along the mustard carpeted hall, automatically touching the wall with his knuckles at every step to prevent any build-up of static in the dry air.

Kate kept her eyes averted as he entered the room, and

Breton felt a slight pang of guilt over his earlier sarcasm.

'That was Carl,' he volunteered. 'He's been working late.'

She nodded uninterestedly, and his guilt instantaneously transformed itself into resentment – not even in the presence of friends would she pretend to care anything about the business. That's the way, Kate, he thought furiously, never ease up for a second. Live well off me, but at the same time reserve the right to despise my work and everybody connected with it.

Breton stared sombrely at his wife and the Palfreys, who were now going back through all the material Miriam had produced, and suddenly realized he was beginning to sway slightly. He retrieved his drink, finished it with one gulp and poured another. I keep on taking this sort of treatment – the old, familiar and repetitious anger patterns began to flow redly on the surface of his mind – but how much is a man supposed to take? I have a wife who complains night and day because I spend too much time at the office, but when I do take an evening off – this is what I get. Phony spiritualists and another king-sized dose of her damned, stinking indifference. To think I wept – yes sir, actually wept with relief – because she was safe that night they found her with Spiedel's brains scattered through her hair. I didn't know it then, but Spiedel was trying to do me a favour. I know it now, though. If only I could . . .

Breton chopped the thought off in alarm as he realized he was setting himself up for a trip.

But he was too late.

Without getting smaller, the subdued orange lights and white-mortared stone chimney of the living-room began to recede into planetary, stellar, galactic distances. He tried to speak, but the transparent overlay of language was shifting across the face of reality, robbing nouns of their significance, making predication impossible. Strange geometries imposed themselves on the perspectives of the room, snapping him sickeningly from pole to alien pole. A face in the group turned towards him – a pale, meaningless free-form – man or woman, friend or enemy? Ponderously, helplessly, over the edge we go . . .

*   *   *

Breton slammed down the hood of the Buick so savagely that the big car moved like a disturbed animal, rocking on its gleaming haunches. In the darkness of its interior Kate was waiting, immobile, Madonna-like – and because she showed no anger, his own became uncontrollable.

'The battery's dead. That settles it – we can't go.'

'Don't be silly, Jack.' Kate got out of the car. 'The Maguires are expecting us – we can phone for a taxi.' Her party clothes were completely inadequate against the night breezes of late October, and she huddled in them with a kind of despairing dignity.

'Don't be so damned reasonable, Kate. We're an hour late already, and I'm not going to a party with my hands like this. We're going back home.'

'That's childish.'

'Thank you.' Breton locked up the car, carelessly smudging the pale blue paintwork with oil from his hands. 'Let's go.'

'I'm going on to the Maguires,' Kate said. 'You can go home and sulk if that's what you want.'

'Don't be stupid. You can't go all the way over there by yourself.'

'I can go by myself and I can get back by myself – I did it all right for years before I met you.'

'I know you've been around, sweetie – I've always been too tactful to mention it, that's all.'

'Thank *you*. Well, at least you won't have the embarrassment of being seen in public with me tonight.'

Hearing the hopelessness creep into her voice, Breton felt a flicker of malicious glee. 'How are you planning to get there? Did you bring any money?'

She hesitated, then held out her hand. 'Give me something for taxi fare, Jack.'

'Not a chance. I'm childish – remember? We're going home.' He savoured her helplessness for a moment, somehow extracting revenge for his own cruelty, then the whole thing fell apart in his hands. This is bad, he thought, even for me. So I arrive late at a party with my face and hands all black – a balanced person would see that as a chance to do an Al Jolson act. Let her ask me just once more and I'll give in and we'll go to the party.

Instead, Kate uttered one short, sharp word – filling him with wounded dismay – and walked away down the street past blazing store windows. With her silvered wrap drawn tight over the flimsy dress, and long legs slimmed even further by needle-heeled sandals, she looked like an idealized screen version of a gangster's moll. For a moment he seemed to see the physical presence of her more clearly than ever before, as though some long-unused focusing mechanism had been operated behind his eyes. The ambient brilliance from the stores projected Kate solidly into his mind, jewel-sharp, and he saw – with the wonder of a brand new discovery – the tiny blue vein behind each of her knees. Breton was overwhelmed by a pang of sheer affection. You can't let Kate walk through the city at night looking like that, a voice told him urgently, but the alternative was to crawl after her, to knuckle under. He hesitated, then turned in the opposite direction, numbed with self-disgust, swearing bitterly.

It was almost two hours later when the police cruiser pulled up outside the house.

Breton, who had been standing at the window, ran heavy-footed to the door and dragged it open. There were two detectives, with darkly hostile eyes, and a backdrop of blue uniformed figures.

One of the detectives flashed a badge. 'Mr John Breton?'

Breton nodded, unable to speak. I'm sorry Kate, he thought, so sorry – come back and we'll go to the party. But at the same time an incredible thing was happening. He could feel a sense of relief growing in one deeply hidden corner of his mind. If she's dead, she's dead. If she's dead, it's all over. If she's dead, I'm free . . .

'I'm Lieutenant Convery. Homicide. Do you mind answering a few questions?'

'No,' Breton said dully. 'You'd better come in.' He led the way into the living-room, and had to make an effort to prevent himself straightening cushions like a nervous housewife.

'You don't seem surprised to see us, Mr Breton,' Convery said slowly. He had a broad, sunburned face and a tiny nose which made scarcely any division between widely spaced blue eyes.

'What do you want, Lieutenant?'

'Do you own a rifle, Mr Breton?'

'Ah . . . yes.' Breton was thunderstruck.

'Do you mind getting it?'

'Look,' Breton said loudly. 'What's going on?'

Convery's eyes were bright, watchful. 'One of the patrolmen will go with you while you get the rifle.'

Breton shrugged and led the way down into his basement workshop. He sensed the patrolman's tenseness as they stepped off the wooden stair on to the concrete floor, so he halted and pointed at the tall cupboard in which he stored a jumble of large tools, fishing rods, archery equipment and his rifle. The patrolman shouldered quickly past him, opened the doors and dragged out the rifle. He had to disengage the sling, which had snagged a fishing reel.

Back in the living-room, Convery took the rifle and rubbed a fingertip in the fine coating of dust which lay over the stock. 'You don't use this much?'

'No. The last time was a couple of years ago. Before I was married.'

'Uh-huh. It's a high velocity job, isn't it?'

'Yes.' Breton could feel the bewilderment building up inside him to an almost physical pressure. What had happened?

'Ugly things,' Convery commented casually. 'They *destroy* animals. I don't know why people use them.'

'It's a good machine, that's all,' Breton replied. 'I like good machines. Oh, I forgot – it isn't working.'

'Why not?'

'I dropped the bolt one day and I think it jammed the pin.'

'Uh-huh.' Convery removed the rifle's bolt, examined it, smelt the breech, peered through the barrel at a table lamp, then handed the weapon back to the patrolman. 'That's the only rifle you own?'

'Yes. Look, Lieutenant, this has gone on long enough. Why are you here?' Breton hesitated. 'Has anything happened to my wife?'

'I thought you'd never ask.' Convery's blue eyes roved Breton's face. 'Your wife is all right. She was foolish enough to walk through the park tonight, without company, and a man attacked her – but she's all right.'

'I don't understand. How ... how can she be all right if she was attacked?'

'Well, she was very lucky, Mr Breton. Another man, who incidentally looked like you, stepped out from behind a tree and blew the attacker's head off with a rifle.'

'*What?* You don't think ... Where's the man now?'

Convery smiled. 'We don't know that, as yet. He seems to have vanished ...'

A sense of aching vastness, shifting of perspectives and parallax, unthinkable transitions in which the curvatures of space-time writhe between negative and positive, and infinity yawns at the mid-point – numinous, illusory, poignant ...

'Look at that guy *drink*,' Gordon Palfrey was saying. 'He's really going into orbit tonight.'

The others turned to look at Breton, who – desperately needing time to reorient himself – smiled wanly and sat down in a deep armchair. He noticed a speculative look in Kate's eyes and wondered if there was any way for a casual observer to detect that he had been blacked out. An analyst called Fusciardi had, after an unsatisfactory investigation, assured him the lapses were unnoticeable, but Breton had found it difficult to believe because the trips often occupied several hours of subjective time. Fusciardi's explanation was that Breton had an unusual, but not unique, capacity for flashes of absolute recall occupying only split seconds of objective time. He had even suggested referring the case to a university psychological team, but at that point Breton had lost interest.

Breton relaxed further into the big old chair, enjoying the comfort of its sane solidity. That particular episode was cropping up more often lately and he found it depressing, even though Fusciardi had warned him that key scenes in his life – especially those involving emotional stress – would be most liable for reclamation. Tonight's trip had been unusually long, and its impact increased by the fact that he had had so little warning. There had been none of the visual disturbances which Fusciardi had told him were commonly the prelude to a migraine attack in other people.

Chilled by his brush with the past, Breton tried to increase his hold on the present, but Kate and the Palfreys were still absorbed in the unusual sample of automatic writing. He listened for a moment as they went through the ritual of trying to identify the author, then allowed his mind to drift in a warm alcoholic haze. A lot seemed to have happened in an evening which had started off in an atmosphere of distilled dullness. I should have stayed in the office with Carl, he thought. The Blundell Cement Company survey had to be completed in less than a week, and had been going slowly even before the unlikely twenty milligal discrepancies in the gravimeter readings showed up. Perhaps they had not been corrected properly. Carl was good, but there were so many factors to be considered in gravity surveying – sun and moon positions, tidal movements, elastic deformation of the Earth's crust, etc. Anybody could make a mistake, even Carl. And anybody could send or receive an anonymous phone call. I was crazy to imagine all those specially engineered connotations – I was caught off balance, that's all. The call was a psychological banana skin and nothing more. Good phrase, that . . . and the whisky's good too. Even the Palfreys are all right if you look at them the right way – especially Miriam. Nice figure. Too bad that she had to let her whole life be influenced by the fact that she was born with that Hollywood Inca MGM Ancient Egyptian priestess face. If she looked like Elizabeth Taylor she could come around here every night . . . Or even Robert Taylor . . .

Feeling himself borne up on a malty cloud of benevolence, Breton tuned in again on the conversation across the room and heard Kate say something about Oscar Wilde.

'Not again,' he protested mildly 'Not Oscar Wilde again!'

Kate ignored him and Miriam smiled her sculptured smile, but Gordon Palfrey was in the mood to talk.

'We aren't *saying* that Oscar Wilde communicated these words, John. But *somebody* did – and the style of some of the stuff is identical to that of Wilde's early prose—'

'His *early* prose,' Breton interrupted. 'That's the point. Let's see – Wilde died about 1900, right? And this is 1981 – so in eighty-one years on the other side, or beyond the veil, or whatever you spiritualists call it, not only has he failed to develop as a writer, but has even slipped back to his undergraduate phase.'

'Yes, but—'

'And it isn't lack of practice, because according to what I've read in those books you lent Kate he's been a favourite with automatic writers since his death. Wilde must be the only author in history whose output went up after he was buried.' Breton laughed, pleased at finding himself in that pleasant transient state of drunkenness in which he always felt able to think and talk twice as fast as when sober.

'You're assuming a one-to-one correspondence between this and any other plane of existence,' Palfrey said. 'But it need not be like that.'

'It mustn't be. From the data you have about the next plane, it seems to be peopled by writers who have no paper or pencils, and who spend their time telepathically projecting drivel down into our plane. And, somehow, Oscar Wilde has become the stakhanovite – possibly as a punishment for writing *De Profundis*.'

Palfrey smiled patiently. 'But we're not *saying* that these . . .'

'Don't argue with him,' Kate said. 'That's what he wants. John's a professional atheist, and he's starting to talk too much anyway.' She shot him a look of scorn but overdid it, making herself look like a little girl for one fleeting second. What an unlikely emotion, Breton thought, to cause rejuvenation.

'She's right,' he said. 'The whole structure of my belief crumbled when I was a kid – the first crack was the discovery that F. W. Woolworth was not a local businessman.'

Kate lit a cigarette. 'He's had ten whiskies. He always pulls that joke when he's had ten.'

And you always pull that one about the ten drinks, Breton thought. You humourless bitch – trying to make me sound like a booze-operated robot. But he remained jovial and talkative, although aware that it was a reaction against the trauma of his trip. He managed to preserve his good spirits right through the coffee and sandwiches stage, and accompanied Kate to the door as she escorted the visitors out to their car.

It was a crisp night in late October, and winter constellations were beginning to climb up beyond the eastern horizon, a reminder that snow would soon come marching down from Canada. Feeling warm and relaxed, Breton lounged in the doorway, smoking his last cigarette of the day while Kate talked to the Palfreys in the car. Two meteorites burned briefly in the sky as he smoked – Journey's end, he thought, welcome to Earth – and finally the car moved off, crunching and spanging in the gravel while its headlights raked through the elms along the drive. Kate waved goodbye and came back into the house, shivering slightly. Breton attempted to put an arm around her as she passed him in the doorway, but she kept walking determinedly, and he remembered his earlier waspishness. The post mortem still had to be held in the small hours, while the bedroom curtains breathed gently in sleep.

Breton shrugged to show himself how little he cared, then flicked the cigarette butt out on to the lawn, where it was extinguished by the dewy grass. He took a final breath of the leaf-scented air and turned to go inside.

'Don't close the door, John.' The voice came from the black-tunnelled shrubbery beside the drive. 'I've come to collect my wife. Had you forgotten?'

'Who's that?' Breton rapped the question out anxiously as the figure of a tall man came towards the light, but he had already recognized the voice. The anonymous phone caller. He felt a surge of dismayed anger.

'Don't you know yet, John?' The stranger reached the

porch, and slowly came up the steps. The overhead light suddenly made his identity very clear.

Breton – transfixed by a vast and inexplicable fear – found himself staring into his own face.

TWO

JACK BRETON DISCOVERED a slight shakiness in his legs as he walked up the steps towards the man called John Breton.

It could, he decided, have been caused by crouching in the draughty, conspiratorial darkness of the shrubbery for more than an hour. But a more likely explanation was that he had not been prepared for seeing Kate again. No amount of forethought or preparation could have cushioned the impact, he realized. The sound of her voice as she said goodbye to the visitors seemed to have flooded his nervous system with powerful harmonics, eliciting new levels of response from his being as a whole, and from the discrete atoms of which it was composed. *I love you,* whispered every molecule of his body, along a billion enzymic pathways. *I love you, Kate.*

'Who are you?' John Breton demanded abruptly. 'What do you want?' He stood squarely in Jack Breton's path, his face a deep-shadowed mask of anxiety in the light from the globe that hung above his head.

Jack Breton fingered the automatic pistol in his overcoat pocket, but – hearing the uncertainty in the other man's voice – he left the catch in the safe position. There was no need to deviate from the plan.

'I've already told you what I want, John,' he said pleasantly. 'And you must know who I am by this time – have you never looked in a mirror?'

'But you look like . . .' John Breton allowed the sentence to tail off, afraid to walk where the words were leading him.

'Let's go indoors,' Jack said impatiently. 'I'm cold.'

He walked forward and was rewarded by the sight of John at once moving backwards, floundering. Afraid of me, Jack Breton thought in mild surprise. This being I created in my own image, this creature who changed my name to John, is afraid of his maker. As he entered the familiar, orange-lit hall, Jack noticed the richness of the carpet underfoot and the almost-tangible feel of money about the old house. The work he had done in the library that day, going through directories and files of local newspapers, had suggested that John Breton was considerably better off than he had been nine years ago, but this was even more pleasant than he had expected. Well done, thou good and faithful servant . . .

'This is far enough,' John Breton said as they reached the spacious living-room. 'I would like some explanations.'

'Well, good for you, *John*.'

Jack surveyed the room as he spoke. The furniture was all new to him, but he remembered the clock and one or two small ornaments. He particularly approved of the deep, high-backed armchairs which had been chosen with no consideration other than comfort in mind. They seemed to extend a welcome to him. Make a mental note, he thought. In spite of the fact that he experiences zero spatial displacement, the time traveller undergoes a substantial psychological dislocation which may manifest itself by the personalization of inanimate objects, eg, armchairs will extend welcomes to him. Be careful!

He returned his attention to John Breton, his natural curiosity reviving now that he was adjusting to the miraculous reality of Kate's existence. His other self was heavier than he ought to be, and dressed in expensively tailored slacks, a maroon sports shirt and cashmere cardigan. Nine years, nine divergent years had made differences, Jack thought. I don't look as sleek as that, or as well fed – but my time is coming. *My* time.

'I'm waiting,' John Breton said.

Jack shrugged. 'I'd have preferred Kate to be here before I went into the spiel, but I guess she's gone upstairs? . . .'

'My wife has gone upstairs.' There was a barely noticeable emphasis on the first two words.

'All right then, John. It's funny, but this is the one part of the whole business I haven't worked out in advance – how to tell you. You see, John – I . . . am . . . you.'

'You mean,' John said with deliberate inanity, 'I'm not myself?'

'No.' He's recovering, Jack Breton thought with reluctant approval, but he's got to take it seriously from the start. He dug deep into his memory.

'John! When you were thirteen, your cousin Louise stayed at your home for most of a summer. She was eighteen, well proportioned. Also she had a bath, regular as clockwork, every Friday night. One afternoon about three weeks after she arrived you took a hand drill from the garage, put a three-thirty-seconds bit in it and drilled a hole in the bathroom ceiling. You drilled it at the widest part of the big Y-shaped crack that Dad never got around to fixing, so it wouldn't be noticed.

'Dad had floored the central area of the roof space for storage, and he had sheeted in the sides, but you found you could move one of the corner panels aside and get over the bathroom. So you took an interest in photography that summer, John, and the roof space made an ideal dark room. Every Friday night – when Louise was in the bath – you went up there into the darkness and soft brown dust. You got over the bathroom and took off—'

'*That's enough!*' John Breton took a step forward, pointing with one finger in baffled accusation. He was trembling slightly.

'Take it easy, John. I'm simply presenting my credentials. Nobody else in the whole world knows the facts I have just mentioned. The only reason I know them is the one I have already given you – I am you. *I* did those things, and I want you to listen to me.'

'I'll have to listen to you now,' John said dully. 'This has been one hell of an evening.'

'That's better.' Jack Breton relaxed a little further. 'Do you mind if I sit down?'

'Go ahead. Do *you* mind if I have a drink?'

'Be my guest.' Jack uttered the words naturally and easily, turning their significance over in his mind. John had been his guest for nine years, as no man had ever been another's guest before – but all that was coming to an end. When they both were seated he leaned forward in the big chair, making his voice cool, calm and reasonable. A lot depended on how he went about the task of making the unbelievable seem believable.

'How do you feel about time travel, John?'

John Breton sipped his drink. 'I feel it's impossible. Nobody could travel forward in time to here and now, because if present-day technology couldn't envisage a time machine, nobody in the past could have built one. And nobody could travel back from the future to the present, because the past is unalterable. That's how I feel about time travel.'

'How about in the other direction?'

'What other direction?'

'Straight across – at right angles to the two directions you've mentioned.'

'Oh, *that*.' John Breton took another drink, almost seeming to be enjoying himself. 'When I was reading science fiction we didn't really class that as honest-to-God time travel. That's probability travel.'

'All right,' Jack said placatingly. 'How do you feel about probability travel?'

'Are you telling me you're from another present? From another time-stream?'

'Yes, John.'

'But, *why*? If it were true, what would bring you here?' John Breton raised the glass to his lips, but did not drink. His eyes were thoughtful. 'Nine years, you said. Is it anything to do with? . . .'

'I heard voices, John.' Kate was standing in the doorway. 'Who have you got with you? Oh . . .'

Jack Breton stood up as she entered the room, and the sight of her filled his eyes, just as it had on the last night he had seen her alive, until her image swamped his awareness – three-dimensional, glowing, perfect. Kate's gaze met his for an instant, then darted away again, and a single star-shell of pleasure burst in his head. He had reached her already. Without saying a word, he had reached her.

'John?' Her voice was tremulous, uncertain. 'John?'

'You'd better sit down, Kate,' John Breton said in a thin, cold monotone. 'I think our friend has a story to tell.'

'Perhaps Kate should have a drink, too,' Jack Breton suggested. 'This is likely to take some time.' Kate was watching him with a wariness he found delicious, and he had to work to keep his voice steady. *She knows, she knows.* While his other self was pouring her a colourless measure, he realized he could be in some danger of making an involuntary trip. He examined his own field of vision and found it clear – no teichopsia, no black star slowly sinking, no fortification phenomena. It appeared safe.

Slowly, carefully, he began marshalling his facts, allowing the past nine years to re-create themselves on the taut canvas of his mind.

THREE

KATE WAS WALKING away down the street, past blazing store windows. With her silvered wrap drawn tight over the flimsy party dress, and long legs slimmed even further by needle-heeled sandals, she looked like an idealized screen version of a gangster's moll. The ambient brilliance from the stores projected her solidly into his mind, jewel-sharp, and he saw – with the wonder of a brand-new discovery – the tiny blue vein behind each of her knees. Breton was overwhelmed by a pang of sheer affection.

You can't let Kate walk through the city at night looking like that, a voice told him urgently, but the alternative was to crawl after her, to knuckle under. He hesitated, then turned in the opposite direction, numbed with self-disgust, swearing bitterly.

It was almost two hours later when the police cruiser pulled up outside the house.

Breton, who had been standing at the window, ran heavy-footed to the door and dragged it open. There were two detectives, with darkly speculative eyes, and a backdrop of blue uniformed figures.

One of the detectives flashed a badge. 'Mr John Breton?'

Breton nodded, unable to speak. I'm sorry, Kate, he thought, so sorry – come back and we'll go to the party.

'I'm Lieutenant Convery. Homicide. Do you mind if I come in?'

'No,' Breton said dully. He led the way into the living-room, and had to make an effort to prevent himself straightening cushions like a nervous housewife.

'I don't quite know how to break this to you, Mr Breton,' Convery said slowly. He had a broad, sunburned face and a tiny nose which made scarcely any division between widely spaced blue eyes.

'What is it, Lieutenant?'

'It's about your wife. It appears she was walking in the park tonight, without company – and she was attacked.'

'Attacked?' Breton felt his knees begin to swim. 'But where is she now? Is she all right?'

Convery shook his head. 'I'm sorry, Mr Breton. She's dead.'

Breton sank down into a chair while the universe heaved and contracted around him like the chambers of a vast heart suddenly exposed. *I did it*, he thought, *I killed my wife*. He was dimly aware of the second detective taking Convery to one side and whispering to him. A few seconds later Convery returned.

'My partner reminds me I've jumped the gun a bit, Mr Breton. Officially, I should have said that the body of a woman had been found with identification on it which suggested she was your wife, but in a clear cut case I don't like prolonging things. Just for the record, have you any reason to believe that the body of a woman of about twenty-five, tall, black-and-gold hair, wearing a silver-blue cocktail dress, we found near the 50th Avenue entrance of the city park, would *not* have been that of Mrs Breton?'

'No reason. She was out alone this evening, dressed like that.' Breton closed his eyes. *I did it – I killed my wife*. 'I let her go alone.'

'We still have to make a positive identification; if you like, one of the patrolmen will drive you to the morgue.'

'It isn't necessary,' Breton said. 'I can do that much.'

The refrigerated drawer rolled out easily on oiled bearings, forming an efficient cantilever, and a stray thought intruded determinedly on Breton's mind. *A good machine*. He looked down at Kate's cold, dreaming face, and at the jewels of moisture curving precisely along her eyebrows. Of its own accord, his right hand moved out to touch her. He saw the blackness of oil rimming the fingernails, and willed his hand to stop. *Thou hast not a stain on thee.*

Lieutenant Convery moved into a corner of his field of vision, close at hand yet light-years away across a universe of pulsating fluorescent brilliance. 'Is this your wife?'

'Who else?' Breton said numbly. 'Who else?'

An indeterminate time later he learned Kate had been clubbed, raped and stabbed. A forensic expert added that they could not be sure of the order in which those things had happened. Breton contained the knowledge of his guilt successfully for a matter of days, while going through senseless formalities, but all the while he knew he was a bomb in which the charge had already ignited, that he was living through the nanoseconds preceding his disintegration into human shrapnel.

It came, with the spurious gentleness of a filmed explosion, on the day after Kate's funeral. He was walking aimlessly through the city's north side, along a street of time-defeated buildings. The day was cold and, although there was no rain, the sidewalks were wet. Near an undistinguished corner he found a clean, new feather and picked it up. It was striped pearly grey and white – dropped by a bird in haste – and he remembered how Kate had worn her clothes like plumage. He looked for a windowsill on which to set the feather, like a single lost glove, and saw a man in shabby denims smiling at him from a doorway. Breton let the feather fall, twinkling and tumbling, on to the greasy concrete and covered it with his foot.

His next action to be guided by his own identity came five weeks later, when he opened his eyes in a hospital bed.

The intervening time was not completely lost to him, but it was flawed and distorted like a scene viewed through pebbled glass. He had been drinking hard, annihilating self-awareness with raw spirit, contracting the frontiers of consciousness. And somewhere in the midst of that kaleidoscope world was born an idea which, to his fevered mind, had all the simplicity of genius.

Psychopathic killers were hard to find, the police had told him. They could not hold out much hope in a case like this. A woman who goes into the park at night alone, they seemed to be saying, what did she *expect*?

Breton had found himself uneasy in their presence, and decided the dismaying thing about the police mentality was that dealing so much with criminals made them aware of another system of morality. Without sympathizing with it, they nevertheless came to understand to some extent, and the needle of their moral compass was deflected. Not their direction – because so long as the amount of bias is known it is still possible to steer – but this, he deduced, was why he felt like a player who did not understand the rules of the game. This was why he was looked at with resentment when he asked what results they were getting – and at some point early in the last weeks he decided to invent new rules.

Kate's murderer had not been seen and, as he had no circumstantial motive for the killing, there was nothing to link him physically to the crime. But, Breton reasoned, there was another kind of connexion. Breton had no way of knowing the killer – *but the killer must know him*. The case had been well covered by the local papers and television services, both of which had carried Breton's picture. It would be impossible for the killer not to have shown interest in the man whose life he had so savagely twisted. And, for a time, Breton came to believe that if he encountered the killer on the street, in the park, in a bar, he would know that man by his eyes.

The city was not large, and it was possible that in his lifetime he had, at one time or another, glimpsed every man in it. Obviously, he had to get into the streets and keep moving, going everywhere that people went, making a rapid playback of a lifetime's exposure to the city's corporate identity – and someday he would look into another man's eyes, and he would *know*. And when that happened . . .

The mirage of hope glimmered crazily in front of Breton for five weeks, until it was finally extinguished by malnutrition and alcoholic poisoning.

He opened his eyes and knew by some quality of the light on the hospital ceiling that there was snow on the ground outside. An unfamiliar emptiness was gnawing at his stomach and he experienced a sane, practical desire for a dish of thick farmhouse soup. Sitting up in the bed he looked around him and discovered he was in a private room, which was barely rescued from complete anonymity by several sprays of deep-red roses. He recognized the favourite flowers of his secretary, Hetty Calder, and there was a vague memory swirl of her long homely face looking down at him with concern. Breton smiled briefly. In the past, Hetty had almost visibly lost weight every time he got a head cold – he hesitated to think how she might have been affected by his performance over the recent weeks.

The desire for food returned with greater force and he reached for the call button.

It was Hetty who, five days later, drove him home from the hospital in his own car.

'Listen, Jack,' she said desperately. 'You've just *got* to come and stay with us for a while. Harry and I would be delighted to have you, and with you not having any family of your own . . .'

'I'll be fine, Hetty,' Breton said. 'Thanks again for the offer, but it's time I went back home and began gathering up the pieces.'

'But will you be all right?' Hetty was driving expertly through the slush-walled streets, handling the big old car as if she were a man, blowing through her cigarette every now and again to send a flaky cylinder of ash on to the floor. Her sallow face was heavy with anxiety.

'I'll be all right,' he said gratefully. 'I can think about Kate now. It hurts like hell, of course, but at least I'm able to accept it. I wasn't able to do that before. It's hard to explain, but I had a feeling there ought to be some government office I could go to – a sort of Department of Death – and explain that there'd been a mistake. That Kate *couldn't* die . . . I'm talking nonsense, Hetty.'

Hetty glanced sideways at him. 'You're talking like a human being, Jack. There's nothing wrong with that.'

'How do I usually talk?'

'Business has been pretty good the last few weeks,' Hetty said crisply. 'You're going to need extra staff.'

She went on to give him a rundown on the new business and the progress that had been made on the existing survey contracts being handled by Breton's engineering consultancy. As she talked he realized he was not as concerned as he ought to be about his business. A gadgeteer by instinct, he had taken a couple of degrees without any real effort because it was the economically sound thing to do, had strayed into the geologically-orientated consultancy, and had taken it over when the owner retired. It had all been so easy, so inevitable, yet vaguely dissatisfying. He had always enjoyed making things, giving rein to the intelligence his hands appeared to possess of their own right, but there seemed to be no time for that now.

Breton huddled in his overcoat, staring nostalgically out at the wet black thoroughfares which were like canals cut through banks of soiled snow. As the car gathered speed, white fluffy chunks of new snow broke upwards from the front end, pounded silently on the windshield and swirled away to the rear, disintegrating, vanishing. He tried to concentrate on

Hetty's words, but saw with dismay that a pinpoint of coloured, shimmering light had been born in the air ahead of him. Not *now,* he thought, rubbing his eyes; but the flickering mote of brilliance was already beginning to grow. Within a minute it was like a brand-new coin spinning, coruscating, remaining in the centre of the field of vision of his right eye no matter which way he turned his head.

'I went over to your place this morning and turned the heat on,' Hetty said. 'At least you'll be warm.'

'Thanks,' he said numbly. 'You go to too much trouble over me.'

The furtive shimmer was growing faster now, blocking out more of his view, beginning to unfold its familiar patterns – restless prismatic geometries, marching, shifting, opening windows into alien dimensions. Not now, he pleaded silently, I don't want to make a trip right now. The optical phenomenon was something he had known since childhood. It could happen at intervals of three months, or of a few days – depending on his degree of mental stress – and was generally preceded by a feeling of unusual well-being. Once the euphoria was past, the zigzag shimmering over the field of his right eye would begin, and that would be followed by one of his inexplicable, frightening trips into the past. The knowledge that each trip took only a fraction of a second of real time, and that it must be some freak of memory, made its imminence no easier to bear – for the scenes he relived were never pleasant. Always, they were segments of his life he would have preferred to forget, crisis points. And it was not hard to guess the particular nightmare which was likely to crop up in the future.

By the time the car reached his house, Breton was effectively blinded on the right side by a beautiful blanket of colour – geometrical, tremulous, prismatic – which made it difficult for him to judge distances accurately. He persuaded Hetty not to get out of the car, waved to her as she moved off down the snow-covered drive, and fumbled open the front door. With the door locked behind him he walked quickly into the living-room and sat down in a deep chair. The shimmering was at its maximum, which meant it would withdraw quite abruptly at any moment, and the trip to God-knows-where would be on. He waited. The vision in his right eye began to clear, he tensed, and the room began to recede, to distort, to exhibit strange perspectives. Ponderously, helplessly, over the edge we go . . .

Kate was walking away down the street, past blazing store windows. With her silvered wrap drawn tight over the flimsy party dress, and long legs slimmed even further by needle-heeled sandals, she looked like an idealized screen version of a gangster's moll. The ambient brilliance from the stores projected her solidly into his mind, jewel-sharp; then he saw – with a vast sense of wrongness – three trees growing in the centre of the street beyond her, right in the traffic lanes, where no trees had ever grown. They were elms, almost stripped of leaves, and something about the configuration of their naked limbs made him want to recoil in loathing. Their trunks, he realized, were insubstantial – automobile headlights were shining right through them. The grouping of the trees was still filling him with dread, yet at the same time he was drawn towards them.

And all the time, Kate was walking away, and a voice was telling him he couldn't let her go through the city at night looking as she did. He fought the same battle with his pride, then turned in the opposite direction, numbed with self-disgust, swearing bitterly . . .

A sense of aching vastness, shifting of perspectives and parallax, unthinkable transitions in which the curvatures of space-time writhe between negative and positive, and infinity yawns at the mid-point – numinous, illusory, poignant . . .

Breton gripped the arms of his chair and held on tightly until the sound of his breathing died away into the silence of the room. He got up, went to the fireplace and wound the old oak-cased clock. The heavy key was cool in his fingers, cool and real. Outside the windows the snow was coming down again in small, dry crumbs, and cars with their lights switched on early ghosted past beyond the trees. The house was filled with patient brown shadows.

He went into the kitchen and began to make coffee while his mind slowly released itself from the stasis induced by the trip. The ensuing lack of nervous energy was another familiar feature of the excursions into the past, but this time the drain had been greater than ever before. Waiting for the water to boil, Breton realized belatedly that the trip had been unusual in other respects – one of them being the introduction of an element of fantasy. Those elm trees growing in the middle of 14th Street had surprised him, but there was more to his sense of shock than an awareness of their incongruity. They had been semi-transparent, like images projected on a more vivid background, but that ragged archway was *real*. He had seen it somewhere, and it meant something – but what?

When the coffee had percolated, he opened the refrigerator and found there was no cream or milk. His stomach moved uneasily at the thought of black coffee, but a search of the depleted kitchen showed that the only other liquid available was in a pickle jar where several pieces of dill swam mistily like surgical specimens. Breton poured a cup of the black brew, flat grey spirals of vapour swirling close to its surface, and went back to the living-room. He sat down, sipped some coffee, and tried vaguely to think about taking control of his personal affairs, but the room was growing dim and he felt tired. One week of treatment and rest had not been enough to repair the damage his extended binge had caused.

Breton awoke in near darkness several hours later. A wan, violet-tinted light was filtering into the room from a street lamp, and tree shadows were moving uneasily on the innermost wall. Repressing a shiver and a surge of self-pity, Breton sat up and decided to go out to eat. As he was getting out of the chair he noticed the vacillating shadow of branches on the dead grey face of the television set – and he remembered where he had seen the three elms.

During a newscast one of the local channels had carried a still photograph of the spot where Kate's body had been found – right by three elms.

The only trouble was that the elms he had seen on his trip had not been frozen to stillness by the camera. They had been moving ... arranging and rearranging their black-etched limbs to the dictates of the night winds. They had been – Breton hesitated before applying the adjective – *real*. Its use meant there had been a shift in his attitude towards the trips, that some part of his mind had found it necessary to believe he had actually seen Kate that very afternoon. Could it be, Breton wondered coldly, that his lonely, guilt-ridden consciousness had defied every law in nature – to travel back through time? Suppose the age-old human desire to do the impossible, to go back into the past and correct mistakes, had been the psychic driving force behind all the trips he had ever made? That would explain why the recreated scenes were always crisis points, times when the course of his life had taken a disastrous turn. Could it be that he was a frustrated time traveller, anchored in the present by the immovable reality of his corporeal body, but managing to release some immaterial aspect of his identity to look back through time and hammer on the invisible walls of the past? If that was the case, then – God help him – he was going to relive that awful, final scene with Kate until he died. And the three elm trees had begun to loom ...

I've got to get out of here, Breton thought, and find a good noisy diner with a juke box, checkered tablecloths, huge vulgar plastic tomatoes on the tables, and normal human beings arguing about the things normal human beings argue about.

He put on lights all over the house, freshened himself up, changed his clothes and was going out through the front door when a slightly shabby sedan swung in the gateway and wallowed up the snow-covered drive. The passenger door opened and Hetty Calder got out, surveyed the snow with obvious disgust, and blew some cigarette ash on to it in a gesture of retaliation.

'Going out? Harry and I came over to see if there was anything we could do.'

'There is.' Breton was amazed at just how much pleasure the sight of her thick, tweedy figure was able to inspire in him.

'You can be my guests at dinner. I'd be glad of your company.'

He got into the rear seat and exchanged brief greetings with Harry Calder, a balding, bookish man of about fifty. The clutter of shopping bags, scarves and magazines around him on the broad seat gave Breton a comforting feeling of being securely back in the world of uncomplicated normalcy. He studied the pre-Christmas store displays as they drove across the city, absorbing every detail, leaving no room for thoughts of Kate.

'How're you feeling now, Jack?' Hetty peered back into Breton's homely little kingdom. 'You didn't look too good when I dropped you off today.'

'Well, I wasn't feeling too wonderful right then, but I'm fine now.'

'What was wrong?' Hetty persisted.

Breton hesitated, and decided to experiment with the truth. 'As a matter of fact, I wasn't seeing very well. Sort of coloured lights had spread over most of my right eye.'

Unexpectedly, Harry Calder turned his head and clucked sympathetically. 'Prismatic, zigzag patterns, eh? So you're another one?'

'Another one? What do you mean, Harry?'

'I get them too – and then the pain starts,' Harry Calder said. 'It's a common preliminary symptom of migraine.'

'Migraine!' Breton felt something heave convulsively in his subconscious. 'But I never get headaches.'

'No? Then you must be one of the lucky ones – what I go through after those pretty colours start marching isn't ordinary. You wouldn't believe it.'

'I never knew there was any connexion between that sort of thing and migraine,' Breton said. 'As you say – I must be one of the lucky ones.'

Even to his own ears, his voice did not carry much conviction.

Breton's belief in the possibility of time travel was born painfully, over a period of months.

He returned to his business, but found himself unable to

make valid judgements on even the most clear-cut administrative issues, while technical decisions had receded to another plane of comprehension altogether. With the assistance of the three staff engineers, Hetty guided the consultancy into something approximating its normal channels of operation. At first, Breton sat at his desk staring at meaningless drawings for hours at a stretch, unable to think of anything but Kate and the part he had played in her death. There were times when he tried to write poetry, to crystallize and perhaps depersonalize his feeling about Kate. The heavy snows of the Montana winter buried the world in silence, and Breton watched it silt across the arrays of parked cars beyond his window. The silence seemed to invade his own body so that he could hear its blind workings, the constant traffic of fluids, the subdividing incursions of air, the patient radial rain of cholesterol in his arteries . . .

And at intervals of six or seven days he made trips, always to that final scene with Kate. Sometimes the elm trees would be so translucent as to be almost nonexistent; at other times they reared up black and real, giving him the impression he would be able to see two figures moving at their bases were it not for the overlaid light of store windows and automobile headlights.

With the continued in-growing of his perceptions, he became more aware of the phenomena he had learned to identify as preludes to the trips. There would be the gradual intensification of his nervous activity, leading him to think he had escaped from despair as it culminated in a heady sense of well-being. Close on that came the first visual disturbances, starting with a furtive glimmer and spreading all over his right eye. As soon as it began to abate, reality *shifted* – and he was back in the past.

The discovery that the visual phenomena were familiar to others surprised Breton, because as a boy he had attempted to describe them to his friends and had never achieved any reaction. Even his parents had shown nothing more than indulgent mock interest and he had never been able to convince them he was not talking about afterimages caused by bright lights. He had learned not to talk about the trips or anything associated with them, and over the years the conviction had grown on him that his experience was unique, private to Jack Breton. But the chance conversation with Harry Calder had changed all that; and the interest it had stirred in him was the only genuine stake he had in the bleak, bitter present.

Breton began spending his afternoons in the public library, aware he was following an idea beside which his former fantasy about Kate's murderer was a working blueprint, but unable to ignore its feverish pounding in his mind. He read the scanty literature on migraine, then went on to general medical works, biographies of famous migraine sufferers, anything his instincts told him might lead in the direction he wanted to go. Never having connected himself with migraine before, Breton had a vague idea it was a recent product of high-pressure civilization. His reading showed him it had been known to ancient cultures, one of them that of the Greeks, who had named it hemicrania – the half-headache. In the great majority of cases, the visual disturbances were followed by severe headaches affecting one side of the head, then nausea. Some people were lucky enough to escape one or other of these symptoms, and there was a rare category of individual who avoided both. Their condition was known as *hemicrania sine dolore*.

One of the most intriguing things as far as Breton was concerned, was the amazing exactness with which his own visual experiences had been described by other men in other times. The medical terms were various – teichopsia, scintillating scotoma – but the one he preferred for its aptness was 'fortification figures'. It had first been used by an eighteenth-century doctor, John Fothergill, who had written:

'... a singular kind of glimmering in the sight, objects swiftly changing their apparent position, surrounded by luminous angles like those of a fortification.'

Fothergill had attributed it to eating too much buttered toast at breakfast time – an explanation Breton found only slightly less satisfactory than up-to-the-minute theories which spoke vaguely about temporary irritations of the visual cortex. One dark brown afternoon, when he and the others in the old building were sitting quietly like objects in the bottom of a petrifying well, he turned the pages of an obscure health magazine and was chilled to find accurate drawings – not of the fortification figures, which would have defeated any artist – but of the black star which sometimes appeared in their place.

One of the drawings was by the French philosopher, Blaise Pascal, and another had been done as far back as the twelfth century by Abbess Hildegarde of Bingen.

'I saw a great star,' the Abbess had written, 'most splendid and beautiful and with an exceeding multitude of falling sparks with which the star followed southwards ... and suddenly they were all annihilated, being turned into black coals and cast into the abyss so that I could see them no more.'

Breton read on quickly but, as was the case with all the other recorded accounts, there was no mention of a subsequent vision of the past. In that respect, it appeared, he really was unique.

A year later Breton pedantically wrote in his notebook:

'I now incline more than ever towards the theory that all migraine sufferers are frustrated time travellers. The power which provides temporal motivation is the desire to return to the past, possibly to relive periods of extreme happiness, but more probably to correct mistakes which are seen in retrospect to have had a malign effect on the course of events.

'Prior to Kate's death my own case was a freakish example of someone who almost *could* go back, not because of greater motivation, but through a lower threshold, a chance configuration of the nervous system. (The visual disturbances may be caused by some degree of temporal displacement of the retina – which is, after all, an extension of the brain, and therefore the sense organ most intimately associated with the activity of the central nervous system.)

'Since Kate's death my retroactive potential has reached an abnormally high level, resulting in frequent trips. Leaving aside the problem of constructing a philosophical edifice capable of accommodating the physical implications, the question remains of how to put theory into practice. Ergotamines, methysergide, diuretics – all these things are in use to minimize the effects of hemicrania, which is hardly what I have in mind ...'

And after five years:

'The monthly cheque from Hetty arrived today. It was larger than usual, making it possible for me to clear my account at the Clermont Scientific Company – which was a relief. I have no wish to impair my credit rating with them at this stage, although I still have the house in reserve and its capital value has appreciated considerably. (What a good idea it was for me to assign formal control of my business to Hetty and that new man Tougher. My only worry is a nagging suspicion that she sometimes augments my cheque with money of her own.)

'There is some cause for excitement today. My work has finally passed from the investigatory to the constructively experimental stage. I could have reached this point sooner but for following several false trails. All of them were suggested by Dr Garnet at the migraine clinic, and I am glad my association with that organization is coming to an end. Prodromal symptoms and cerebral blood flow, response to various drugs, metabolism of the amines – red herrings, the lot of them. (As far as my work is concerned, anyway. I must not be too unkind to Garnet.)

'To think that my big breakthrough came as a result of using a badly designed screwdriver!

'I don't know what prompted me to withdraw the fluid from that huge blister on the palm of my right hand, unless it was that I had been thinking a lot about the possible use of hemicranial pain as a trigger mechanism to augment chronomotive impulses. Work at the clinic had established that a substance called kinin was produced in the region of the head arteries during migraine attacks in people not fortunate enough to be afflicted with *hemicrania sine dolore*.

'Blister fluid itself does not cause pain, but I have proved that when it **is** withdrawn and put in contact with glass it develops kinin, which – when put into the blister again –

certainly does cause pain. By injecting kinin at the first onset of teichopsia heralding my last three trips I was able to experience genuine hemicrania, and – for the first time – I *heard* those three elm trees moving in the wind!

'That phase of my work is now complete, and I now am faced with the problem of effecting the temporal displacement of a considerable physical mass, ie, my own body. Vast amplification of neural impulses will be required, and I have an uneasy premonition I may have to look for some loophole in Kirchoff's Laws.

'However, I am in a mood of supreme confidence. I must calm down, though, in case I precipitate another trip. Excitement is a traditional trigger factor in hemicrania. Somewhere I have a note of a comment by the French patriot Dr Edward Liveing who, in 1873, said – "We all know that it is not everyone who can with impunity, do himself the pleasure of assisting at certain theatrical representations where the glory of France is daily celebrated with noise and smoke . . ." '

And after a further three years:

'Abrogation of Kirchoff's Laws was almost easier than I had expected – consideration of the fourth dimension makes so many things possible – but I had seriously underestimated the expense. The sale of the house and furniture raised only a fraction of the money I needed. Fortunately, I was able to persuade Hetty and Carl Tougher to void our agreement of the last eight years in favour of an outright sale. They are worried about me, especially Hetty, but I think I have convinced them of both my sanity and my physical well-being. Hetty has got noticeably older, though, and she smokes too much.

'Kate, my darling, this is the last time I will address you through the medium of this notebook. The time is not too distant, however, when we shall be able to turn its pages together. Until then, my love, until then . . .'

Breton waited till dusk before he went to the park.

He stopped the now-aged blue Buick several hundred yards

from the 50th Avenue entrance and spent a few minutes checking over the equipment. The hat came first. It was lying on the rear seat, looking very much like any other slightly shabby hat, except that occasional flickers of orange light escaped from under its brim. He picked it up, positioned it carefully on his head and spent some time connecting the leads which projected down from the sweat band to others which emerged from under his shirt collar. When the connexions were completed, he turned up the collar of his raincoat and moved his limbs experimentally. The network of wires taped to his body dragged painfully at his skin, but he had what amounted to complete freedom of movement.

Breton turned his attention to the rifle. When moving his personal belongings out of the house he had found the weapon lying in the basement cupboard, coated in white dust, and had brought it to his newly rented apartment on the east side. On checking it over, he had discovered the firing pin was jammed – the result of some forgotten accident – and had paid a gunsmith to put it right. The slim lines of the rifle were marred by the bulk of the infra-red sight he had added for use in darkness. Breton filled the ammunition clip with cool brass cylinders from his pocket, latched it on to the rifle and bolted the first cartridge up into the breech. There was a possibility he would get as little as two seconds to find his mark, aim and fire – and he did not want to waste any of his meagre ration of time.

He sat motionless for a few minutes, waiting for the immediate vicinity to empty of pedestrians. It was almost a week since his last trip, and he could feel that the time was right. His veins were coursing with excitement – one of the basic hemicranial trigger factors – and the electrical activity in his brain was higher than normal, producing a kind of taut exultation. The almost psychedelic change in perception, familiar to migraine sufferers as the first symptom of a new onslaught, was influencing his awareness, ringing everyday objects with a halo of imminence – sadness, lurking peril, intoxication. As soon as the block was clear, Breton got out of the car, withdrew the rifle and closed his raincoat around it, grasping the stock through the slit pocket. Night breezes tugged at him from many directions, exploring his form like blind men's fingers while he walked awkwardly with the concealed burden.

As he neared the 50th Avenue entrance, the first visual disturbances began. A fugitive glimmer of light trembled in the field of his right eye and slowly spread, exhibiting its prismatic complexities. Breton was reminded of a swarm of water beetles, tumbling on each other, splitting sunlight with the movement of their oily bronze backs. He was glad it was not the falling black star; the fortification figures took longer to develop, giving him more time.

Breton went into the park and headed towards its centre along paths on which dry fallen leaves rolled with metallic crackles. A few people, mostly couples, were sitting on benches near the lighted paths, but he veered away across the grassy central area and was swallowed by the anonymous darkness in a matter of seconds. He brought the rifle out from under his coat and self-consciously raised it to his face to check the infra-red scope, but his right eye was dazzled with marching colours and he remembered he had no choice other than to trust his previous zeroing-in work. The blanket of living brilliance was nearing its maximum when he found the three elms.

He went to within thirty yards of the triangular group, twisted his left arm through the rifle's broad leather sling and dropped down on one knee in the classical marksman's position. The damp earth made an oval patch of coldness on his leg. I must be crazy, he thought, but he could hear himself whispering Kate's name over and over again. He touched the brim of his hat and a low humming sound came from it as the high-efficiency batteries strapped to his body began delivering power. Simultaneously, the hypodermic gun built into the circuit fired a cloud of kinin into the shaven patch above his right temple. He felt its icy sting, then agony coiled languorously through his head as the chemical spread in the cerebral arteries. Breton noted abstractedly that there were no people about – all his painstaking work to produce an arrangement which would not attract too much attention had been quite unnecessary – then the sheet of prismatic geometries began to shrink, abruptly. It was time.

'Kate!' he screamed. '*Kate!*'

She was moving uncertainly through the darkness, her pale blue dress and silvered wrap glimmering as though by their own phosphorescence. A black shape moved from under the ragged archway of the elm trees, keening unhappily, like a loathsome bird of prey. It closed with Kate, arms upraised, and she sobbed once with fear. Breton put the thick crosshairs on to the black silhouette, but his finger hesitated on the trigger. Their bodies were close together – suppose the bullet passed right through both? He raised his left arm a fraction and fired instinctively as the crosshairs intersected fleetingly on the head. The rifle jarred against his shoulder, and the dark head was no longer a head . . .

Brenton lay for a long time with his face pressed down into a microcosm of grassy roots. Under his left hand the rifle barrel grew warm from the single shot, then cooled again, and still he was unable to move. He was in the grip of an exhaustion so intense that each thought required eons of dogged effort to drive it through to completion. How long, he wondered, have I been lying here? The fear that somebody would come along and find him lying there nagged at him incessantly, gradually reaching a thundering urgency, but he might as well have been trapped in a dead body.

His mind, too, felt different. Pressures had been relieved, potentials had been discharged by the fantastic cerebral orgasm of the trip. *The big trip*. He had made it – the thought brought a flicker of satisfaction – eight years of continuous work had had their brief reward. He had breasted the implacable river of time and—

Kate!

The incredible realization fountained through him, bringing the first involuntary movement of his limbs. He brought his hands up under his shoulders and pressed hard against the ground. The process of getting to his feet was an extended one, involving getting his arms to raise his body, resting on his heels, then grimly forcing his legs to accept weight. He unslung the rifle, put it under his coat and began to walk. There was nobody near the three elm trees, but this was not surprising. The man he had shot would have been found and taken away eight years earlier, and as for Kate – she must be at the house. A woman's place is in the home, he thought inanely as he began to run, swaying grotesquely as his knees orbited at every step. His wild elation lasted until he was close to the park's entrance, and could see the milk-white globes on their twin pillars. Until a thought ended it.

But, a voice suddenly whispered, *if Kate's at home – why are you out in the park with a rifle?*

If she's alive – how can you remember her funeral?

Later, while sanity still lingered, he drove past the house. The new owners had not yet moved in, and the FOR SALE sign was still standing in the garden, reflecting stray beams from the street lights. Breton experienced a yearning impulse to go into the house and make sure, but instead he pressed down hard on the gas pedal. The old Buick faltered for a moment, then surged away down the quiet avenue. There were lights in all the other houses.

Breton drove to a bar on the city's north side, right on the edge of the prairie, where tumbleweeds sometimes came nuzzling at the door like hungry dogs. Seated at the long bar, he ordered a whisky – his first since the nightmare binge of eight years earlier – and stared into its amber infinities. Why had he not deduced what was bound to happen? Why had his mind gone so far along its lonely road, only to stop short of the final, obvious step?

He *had* gone back in time, he *had* shot a man – but nothing was going to alter the reality of Kate's death. Breton dipped a finger in the whisky and drew a straight line on the smooth plastic of the bar top. He stared at it for a moment, then added another line forking out from the first. If the first line represented the stream of time as he knew it, and in which nothing had changed, then the few seconds he had wrested from the past had taken place on the divergent line. When his brief moment of death-dealing was over, he had snapped back to the present in his own time-stream. Instead of bringing Kate back to life in his own line he had prevented her death in the divergent track.

Breton took another sip from his glass, trying to assimilate the idea that *somewhere* Kate was alive. He looked at his watch. Almost midnight. Kate might be in bed, or having a last cup of coffee with her husband – the other Jack Breton. For Breton's trip into the past had, when it set up a new time-stream, created another universe in its entirety, complete with a duplicate of himself. That other universe would have its own cities, lands and oceans, planets and stars, receding galaxies – but none of these things were important beside the fact that he had bought Kate another life, only to have her share it with another man. And it was wrong to say that the other man was himself, because an individual is the sum of his experiences, and that other Breton had not looked on Kate's dead face, endured the guilt, or surrendered eight years of his life to the monomania which had recreated Kate Breton.

The forked line he had drawn on the bar was fading away into the air. Breton stared at it sombrely. He had a feeling he had used up something inside himself, that he would never again be able to summon up the vast chronomotive potential which had hurled him back through the barriers of time. But supposing . . .

He wet his finger again, made a fresh dot to mark the present on the line representing the main time-stream, and matched it with a similar dot on the divergent line. After a moment's thought, he drew a heavy lateral stroke connecting the two.

Suddenly he understood why the deeply-buried but ever-watchful part of his mind that controlled these times had allowed him to continue on the path he had chosen eight years earlier. He had defied time itself to create another Kate, and that was a far greater task than the one which lay before him now.

All he had to do was reach her.

FOUR

IT WAS LONG past midnight before Jack Breton stopped talking, but he knew they were just about convinced.

Somewhere along the way John Breton and Kate had begun to believe him – which was why it was so important to go carefully, not risk losing their trust. This far, everything he had told them had been true, but now the lies would begin and he had to avoid falling into his own trap. He sat back in the deep chair and looked at Kate. There had been almost no physical change in the past nine years, except for her eyes, and the way in which she had acquired conscious control of her own beauty.

'This must be a trick,' Kate said tensely, not wanting to surrender normalcy without a fight. 'Everybody has a double somewhere.'

'How do you know?' Both Bretons spoke at once, in perfect synchronization, and glanced at each other while Kate seemed to grow pale, as though the coincidence had proved something to her.

'Well, I read it ...'

'Kate's a student of the funny papers,' John interrupted. 'If a thing happens independently to Superman *and* Dick Tracy, then it must be true. It stands to reason.'

'Don't speak to her like that,' Jack said evenly, suppressing sudden anger at his other self's attitude. 'It isn't an easy thing to swallow first time around without proof. You should know that, John.'

'Proof?' Kate was immediately interested. 'What proof can there be?'

'Fingerprints, for one thing,' Jack said, 'but that calls for equipment. Memories are easier. I told John something that nobody else in the world knows.'

'I see. Then I ought to be able to test you the same way?'

'Yes.' His voice was shaded with sudden doubt.

'All right. John and I went to Lake Louise for our honeymoon. On the day we left there, we went to an Indian souvenir place and bought some rugs.'

'Of course we did,' Jack replied, laying the faintest stress on the pronoun. 'That's one of them over by the window.'

'But there was more. The old woman who ran the store gave me something else, free of charge, because we were on our honeymoon. What was it?' Kate's face was intent.

'I ...' Jack floundered, wondering what had gone wrong. She had beaten him, effortlessly. 'I can't remember – but that doesn't prove anything.'

'Doesn't it?' Kate stared at him triumphantly. 'Doesn't it?'

'No, it doesn't,' John Breton put in. 'I can't remember that episode either, honey. I don't remember that old stick giving us anything.' He sounded regretful.

'John!' Kate turned to him. 'That tiny pair of moccasins – for a baby.'

'I still don't remember. I've never seen them around.'

'We never had a baby, did we?'

'That's the advantage of family planning.' John Breton smirked drunkenly into his glass. 'You don't have any family.'

'Your jokes,' Kate said bitterly. 'Your indestructible, polyeurethane jokes.'

Jack listened with a peculiar sense of dismay. He had created these two people as surely as if he had stalked the Earth amid Biblical lightnings and breathed life into handfuls of clay, yet they had lived *independently*. For nine years, he thought, with an indefinable feeling of having been cheated. He fingered the oily metal of the pistol in his pocket.

John Breton flicked the rim of his empty glass, making silvery ringing sounds. 'The point is that we know this man is telling the truth. I can see myself sitting over there; *you* can see me sitting over there. Look at that tie clip he's wearing – I'll bet it's that gold wire one you made at that jewellery class you went to before we were married. Is it ... Jack?'

Jack Breton nodded. He opened the worn clip and reached it across to Kate. She hesitated, then took it from him in such a way that their hands did not touch. Her eyes narrowed with a look of incongruous professionalism as she held the clip up to the light and a pang of affection checked his breathing. She stood up abruptly and left the room, leaving the two men facing each other across an open hearth with its dying, whitening logs.

'There's more to tell, isn't there?' John Breton sounded carefully casual.

'Yes. It took another year to modify the chronomotor to make it possible for me to travel across time. There's a negligible amount of power involved, but the demand is continuous. I think that to get here I had to travel back in time for perhaps a millionth of a second – which is, of course, just as "impossible" as going back for a year – thus causing a kind of temporal ricochet into—'

'That's not what I mean,' John cut in. 'I'm asking you what your plans are. What happens next?'

'Well, what do you think *ought* to happen? As I told you earlier tonight – you're living here with my wife, and I want her back.' Jack Breton watched his other self carefully, and saw that his reaction was surprisingly small.

'But Kate is my wife. You told us yourself that you let your wife go out and get murdered.'

'And so did you, John. But it was *I* who gave up nine years to finding a way to go back and correct your mistake. Don't forget that, old friend.'

John Breton's mouth tightened obstinately. 'There's something terribly wrong with your reasoning there, but I still want to know what happens next. Have you got a gun in your pocket?'

'Of course not,' Jack said quickly. 'I couldn't think of shooting you, John. It'd be like shooting myself.' He paused, listening to the sound of Kate upstairs opening and slamming drawers. 'No, we have an eternal triangle here, and the only reasonable way to resolve it is for the lady concerned to choose one corner or the other.'

'Some choice!'

'But it *is* a real choice, John. Nine years have changed us both. We're two different men, each with a claim on Kate. I want to stay here for a week or so, to let her get used to the idea, and then ...'

'You're crazy! You can't just move in on us like that!'

John Breton's sudden anger surprised Jack. 'But why not? It seems a reasonable proposition to me.'

'Reasonable! You appear out of the blue ...'

'I appeared out of the blue once before, and Kate was glad of it then,' Jack interrupted. 'Maybe I still have something to offer her. You two don't seem to be hitting it off too well.'

'That's our business.'

'I agree – yours and Kate's and mine. Our business, John.'

John Breton jumped to his feet, but Kate came into the room before he could speak. He turned his back to her and began kicking the burnt-out logs, sending topaz sparks twisting up into the darkness of the chimney.

'I found it,' Kate said quietly. She held out both hands, showing an identical gold tie clip in each. 'They are the same, John. And I know my own work.'

'How do you like that?' John Breton spoke bitterly to the coloured stones of the fireplace. 'The tie clip convinced her. Anybody could rustle up a good facsimile of *me* – that meant nothing – but she knew nobody could reproduce a complicated thing like her Goddam tie clip.'

'This is no time to be childish.' Kate stared at John's back, wasting one of her exaggerated looks of scorn on it.

'We're all tired,' Jack said. 'I could use some sleep.'

Kate hesitantly crossed the room towards him, holding out his clip. Their fingers touched momentarily as he took it, swamping him with a fierce yearning to wrap his arms around her achingly familiar body with its taut, horizontally wrinkled silks. Their eyes met and locked for an instant, forming an invisible axis around which the rest of the universe seemed to seethe like clouds in a whirlwind. Before she turned away, he thought he glimpsed in her face all the compassion and forgiveness he had needed so desperately for the past nine years.

Later, he stood at the window of the guest room, listening to the old house settling down for what was left of the night. One week, he thought. That's how long I'm prepared to wait. By that time I should be able to step into John Breton's shoes without anyone – apart from Kate – being able to tell the difference.

As he was turning away from the window, the night sky was suddenly splintered into starry fragments by a shower of criss-crossing meteors. He got into bed and tried to sleep, but he found himself watching – with a strange uneasiness – for further shooting stars.

Finally, he got up, pulled the drapes and allowed himself to sink into the warm, black ocean of sleep.

FIVE

JOHN BRETON OPENED his eyes slowly and stared through dim amber light, waiting – with a kind of pleasant terror – for the onrushing tides of identity to return to him. (There's a rectangle of pale luminosity: what is it? Bedroom window in dim light? Some unfamiliar aspect of disembodied soul? Movie screen? Extra-dimensional doorway?) He was sometimes convinced that each night's sleep brought a dissolving of personality, and that its accurate reformation in the morning depended entirely on his being given the right clues. If he woke up in different surroundings, with different possessions – then he could take up another life altogether, with nothing more than an uneasy suspicion that something had gone wrong.

There was a movement in the bed beside him and he turned towards it. Kate's dreaming face . . .

Breton came fully awake, remembering the previous night and the arrival of Jack Breton. The man was a thinner, shabbier, more intense version of himself. He was a cipher, a flawed human being who apparently saw nothing strange in the idea of asking a man and his wife to accept him into their home, and presenting them with such a preposterous scheme.

So Kate was supposed to choose one or the other!

Breton tried to recall why he had not driven his fist into the familiar face. He had been drunk, of course, but there was more to it than that. Was it something to do with the way in which Kate had seemed to accept the idea, while pretending not to take it too seriously?

Or was it that the fantastic scheme somehow dovetailed into the flaws in their marriage? Kate and he had been together for eleven years, during which time they had seen their ups and downs, and an even more significant motion – the drifting apart. The only way they could reach each other now was by wielding longer and longer knives. It seemed that the more money he made, the more Kate needed; so he worked even harder, while she became more distant and indifferent. A frigid, sterile escalation.

The arrival of Jack Breton could mean an effortless and guilt-free escape. Kate and Jack could go away together, or – the idea gusted coolly through Breton's mind – *he* could bow out of the situation and leave them to it. He could take some money and go anywhere – Europe, South America, there was even the Moon. Buzz Silvera's last letters from Florida had as good as said they were taking any competent practical engineer who was prepared to go.

Breton was lying in his fleecy tunnel of warmth, bemusedly trying the concept on for size, when the tardy intellectual realization came that his other self had not been part of a dream. He would have to be faced, all day and for many days to come. Shivering slightly, Breton got out of bed, put on his dressing-gown and went down for breakfast.

Kate Breton kept her eyes closed until John had left the room; then, without getting up, she made walking movements with her legs until the sheets were a crumpled mound at the foot of the bed, and she was lying naked, paralleling the greyed white plane of the ceiling. She lay still for a moment, wondering if John was in the shower or if he had gone downstairs. He might come back into the room and see her lying in self-conscious nudity, but that would be a non-event. ('Anthropologically speaking, you're not quite right,' he had said reflectively, only a month earlier. 'The female is characterized by conical things – and yours are cylindrical.')

Jack Breton would not have said anything like that, Kate thought, remembering the thin, shabby figure with the eyes of a latter-day Swinburne. The man projected emotion with silent-screen intensity, but – although she had mentally dissociated herself – she had felt the responses begin within her, pervasive and unstoppable. Jack Breton was almost the archetype of the Romance hero, sacrificing his life to an unattainable vision. And behind that pain-shadowed face was *something* which had driven him to challenge and conquer Time itself, for the sake of her, Kate Breton. I have become unique, she thought gratefully.

The feeling of excitement centring around her like an emotional cyclone grew even stronger, triggering slow undulations in her torso. Kate got up and stared at herself with speculative eyes in the long mirror.

Jack Breton stood at the window of the guest bedroom, gazing out at a world dressed in its morning greys. The Time B world. It occurred to him that there must be visible differences in the two time-streams, apart from the vital one of Kate's existence. In this world a psychopathic killer had died in strange circumstances, which would have altered some things – especially for the future victims he never got around to. There was also the fact that in the Time B world the Breton engineering consultancy had prospered in John Breton's hands, giving him the chance to influence events in possibly significant ways. Jack reminded himself to watch out for differences and get used to them quickly, so that he could step into John Breton's shoes with as little fuss as possible.

He frowned at the dark, stolid beeches in the back garden as he considered the disposal of the body. Apart from the purely mechanical problem, there was the more delicate question of Kate's reaction. If she ever suspected, for even an instant, that he had murdered John it would be the end. She would have to believe that John had agreed to vanish from her life, or – if that could not be arranged – that he had died in an accident.

Jack's eyes suddenly focused on a small silvery dome which could be seen beyond the line of beech trees. So John had got around to building a proper observatory in the garden – that was a thing *he* had always wanted to do and had never managed to find the time. His other self had done it, though. His other self had gone on ahead with Kate and done lots of things.

Feeling cold and lonely, Jack Breton stood at the window a moment longer, then became aware of movement in other parts of the house. There was a faint smell of coffee and frying ham in the air. He went out of the bedroom, down the long stairs and into the kitchen. Although it was very early, Kate was fully dressed and groomed, wearing a brushed wool *café au lait* sweater and white skirt. She was laying plates on the kitchen table as Jack came through the door. The sight of her stilled his heart, then sent it into a series of great, lumping spasms.

'Good morning, Kate,' he said. 'Anything I can do to help?'

'Oh ... hello. No, thanks.' He saw tinges of pink appear over her cheekbones.

'But you shouldn't have to spend your time on housework,' he said with mock gallantry.

'You can set your mind at ease on that score,' John Breton said from near the window, and Jack suddenly became aware of his dressing-gowned appearance. 'We have a cook-housekeeper who acts as a bulwark between Kate and the necessities of domestic life. What time does Mrs Fitz get here, anyway?'

'She won't be coming,' Kate answered tartly. 'I called and told her we wouldn't need her for a few days.'

John appeared not to hear. He was leaning on the window ledge with his ear close to a radio, apparently waiting for something. Jack ignored him and turned back to Kate.

'There you are!' He smiled. 'You wouldn't have to do it if I wasn't here. I'm *entitled* to help.'

'It's all ready. Please sit down.'

Kate's eyes met his briefly and he almost reached out to take what was his. Instead, he sat compliantly at the table while all his instincts protested their frustration. The exhaustion of the previous night had lifted, and once again his mind was filled with the wonder of Kate's existence. She was alive, warm, real; in the aura of her emotional significance more miraculous than all the starry infinities of the Time B universe . . .

John Breton's fingers suddenly spun the volume control on the radio and the voice of a newscaster washed through the kitchen, causing Kate to frown at him.

'Do we need that radio so loud?'

'Keep quiet a minute.'

'I don't see why—'

'Just keep *quiet*!' John twisted the control to its limit and the announcer's voice boomed out, rippled with electronic distortions.

'. . . now continuing in the eastern hemisphere. A spokesman for the Mount Palomar observatory said the meteor display was already the most brilliant in history, and was showing no signs of slackening off. Televised reports from Tokyo – where the meteor display is now at its height – will be available on major networks as soon as the malfunctioning of the communications satellites, which developed a few hours ago, has been corrected.

'Mr C. J. Oxtoby, president of Ustel – the major satellite operating agency – has denied an early report that the Courier satellites were drifting out of the synchronous orbit. Another possible explanation for the communications failure of last night – which has already led to the filing of massive compensation claims by a number of civil users – is that the satellites have suffered meteor damage.

'And now, on the local scene, fierce objections to the one-way street system proposed . . .'

John Breton turned the radio off.

'The world still goes on,' he said with a hint of challenge in his voice, somehow excusing himself for not having had anything important to say on the subject of the John-Kate-Jack triangle. Jack briefly wondered to whom the apology was addressed.

'Of course it does. The world does still go on. Have some breakfast and don't think about it too much.' Jack felt a macrocosmic amusement at his other self's preoccupation with trivia.

'I don't like those meteors,' John said as he sat down. 'Yesterday was one hell of a day. A gravimetric survey goes haywire, the Palfreys arrive. I drink a ruinous quantity of Scotch I don't even want, I take the longest trip for years, even the sky starts to play tricks, and then . . .'

'To cap it all, I show up,' Jack completed. 'I know it's tough on you, but don't forget I have every right to be here. We settled all that last night.'

'*You* settled it,' John muttered ungraciously. 'I don't see how I can even talk this thing over with Kate while you're hanging around us.'

'What is there to talk over?' Jack Breton ate steadily as he spoke, enjoying himself.

John's fork clattered to his plate. He sat with hunched shoulders for a moment, looking down at it, then raised his eyes to Kate in a level stare of disgust.

'Well, how about it? Have you weighed up our various merits and demerits yet?'

'Don't look at me like that.' Kate's voice was taut with anger. 'You're the man around this house – if you don't like Jack being here why don't you do something positive about it?'

'Positive? You're the one that's in a position to do something positive – he said so himself. All you've to do is tell him to leave because you would prefer to go on living with me. What could be easier?'

'You seem to be trying to make it difficult,' Kate said slowly. 'Are you doing it deliberately?'

'Very good, Kate,' John commented, abruptly recovering his composure. 'I like the way you turned that one around. Very neat.'

Kate's lips moved soundlessly as she raised a bottle-green coffee cup to her mouth, shooting him one of her exaggerated, schoolgirl looks of scorn over the rim. How odd, Jack thought, that a negative emotion like scorn should have the power to make her seem younger.

John Breton pushed his food away and got to his feet. 'Sorry to break this up, but somebody around here has to work.'

'You aren't going to the office!' Kate sounded shocked.

'I've got to – besides, you two will have lots to talk about.'

Jack concealed his amazement at the other man's seeming indifference to how near he was to losing Kate. 'Do you have to go? Why not let Hetty handle things for a few days?'

John frowned. 'Hetty? Hetty who?'

'Hetty Calder, of course.' Cool vapours of unease swirled momentarily in Jack's chest as he saw the perplexed look on John's face. This was supposed to be a duplicate world, perfect in every detail. How could John Breton have any difficulty in placing Hetty Calder?

'Oh, *Hetty*! It's been so long, I'd almost forgotten. She's been dead for seven or eight years.'

'How? ...'

'Lung cancer, I think it was.'

'But I saw her just a week or so ago. She was all right – and still smoking two packs a day.'

'Perhaps she changed her brand in your world.' John shrugged casually, and in that instant Jack hated him.

'Isn't that strange?' Kate spoke in a child's wondering voice. 'To think that funny little woman's alive, somewhere, going about her business and not knowing we've already attended her funeral, not knowing she's really dead.'

Jack Breton experienced an urge to correct Kate, but was unable to find any suitable grounds. If Kate was really alive, then Hetty was really dead – it was all part of the deal. He sipped hot coffee, surprised at the strength of the regrets conjured up by the memory of Hetty's homely, capable face breathing through its centrally-mounted cigarette.

'I'm going to get dressed.' John Breton hesitated at the door as if about to say something further, then went out of the kitchen, leaving Jack alone with Kate for the first time. The air was warm, and prisms of pale sunlight slanted from the curtained windows. A pulsing silence filled the room as Kate toyed desperately with her food, looking slightly distraught and out-of-place against the background of cosy domesticity. She took a cigarette and lit it. Breton's awareness of her was so intense that he could hear the tobacco and rice paper burning as she drew on the smoke.

'I think I arrived at just the right time,' he said finally.

'Why's that?' She avoided looking at him.

'You and ... John are about ready to split up, aren't you?'

'That's putting it a little strongly.'

'Come on, Kate,' he urged. 'I've *seen* the two of you. It was never like this with us.'

Kate looked fully at him and he saw the uncertainty in her eyes.

'No? I don't understand this Time A and Time B thing very well, Jack, but up until that night in the park you and John were the same person. Right?'

'Right.'

'Well, we had fights and arguments then, too. I mean, it was *you* – as well as John – who refused to give me taxi fare and—'

'Don't, Kate!' Breton struggled to make his mind encompass what she was saying. She was right, of course, but during the last nine years he had avoided some avenues of memory, and he was strangely reluctant to be forced to explore them now. The dream could not sustain the dichotomy.

'I'm sorry – perhaps that wasn't fair.' Kate tried to smile. 'None of us seem to be able to shake off that particular episode. And there's Lieutenant Convery ...'

'Convery! Where does he come in?' Breton's senses were alerted.

'The man who attacked me was called Spiedel. Lieutenant Convery was in charge of the investigations into his death.' Kate looked sombrely at Breton. 'Did you know you were seen that night?'

'I hadn't thought about it.'

'You were. Half a dozen teenagers who must have been having a communal roll in the grass told the police about seeing a man with a rifle who materialized almost on top of them and vanished just as quickly. Naturally enough, the description they were able to give fitted John. To be honest, until last night I always had an illogical feeling it had been John – although the investigation cleared him completely. Several of our neighbours had seen him standing at the window, and his rifle was broken anyway.'

Breton nodded thoughtfully, suddenly aware of how near he had come to saving Kate and getting rid of the Time B Breton at one stroke. So the police had tried to pin the shooting on John! What a pity the dictates of chronomotive physics had caused the bullet which killed Spiedel to snap back into Time A along with the rifle and the man who had fired it. The rifling marks on it would have matched those produced by John Breton's unfired and broken rifle – which would have given the omnipotent ballistics experts something to think about.

'I still don't see what you mean about Convery,' he said aloud. 'You said John was cleared.'

'He was, but Lieutenant Convery kept on coming around here. He still calls when he's in the district, and drinks coffee and talks to John about geology and fossils.'

'Sounds harmless.'

'Oh, it is. John likes him, but he reminds me of something I don't want to remember.'

Breton reached across the table and took Kate's hand. 'What do I remind you of?'

Kate moved uneasily, but kept her hand in his. 'Something I do want to remember, perhaps.'

'You're my wife, Kate – and I want you back.' He felt her fingers interlock with his then grow tighter and tighter as though in some trial of strength. Her face was that of a woman in childbirth. They sat that way, without speaking, until John Breton's footsteps sounded outside the kitchen door. He came in, now wearing a grey business suit, and went straight to the radio.

'I'll get the latest news, before I go.'

'I'll tidy up here,' Kate said. She began clearing the table.

Jack Breton stood up, aware of an overwhelming resentment at his other self's presence in the house, and walked slowly through the house until he was standing in the tranquil silence of the living-room. Kate had responded to *him* – and that was important. It was why it had been necessary for him to do it this way, to walk straight in on Kate and John and explain everything to them.

A more logical and efficient method would have been to keep his presence in the Time B world a secret; to murder John, dispose of the body and quietly take over his life. But then he would have been burdened with a sense of having cheated Kate, whereas now he had the ultimate justification of knowing she preferred him to the man the Time B Breton had come to be. That mattered very much, and now it was time to think in detail about his next step – the elimination of John Breton.

Frowning in concentration, Jack Breton moved about the living-room, absentmindedly lifting books and small ornaments, examining them and carefully putting everything back in its original place. His attention was caught by a sheaf of closely-written squares of white paper, the top one of which had an intricate circular pattern on it. He lifted the uppermost sheet and saw that what he had taken to be a pattern was actually handwriting in a finely-executed spiral. Breton rotated the paper and slowly read a fragment of poetry.

I have wished for you a thousand nights,
While the green-glow hour-hand slowly veers.
I could weep for the very need of you,
But you wouldn't taste my tears.

He had set the sheet down and was turning away from the table when the significance of the lines speared into him. It took several seconds for the floodgates of memory to open, and when they did his forehead prickled icily with fear. He had written these words himself during the period of near-madness following Kate's death – but he had never shown them to anyone.

And that had been in another world, and another time.

SIX

JOHN BRETON MADE several abortive attempts to leave for his office, but each time returned to pick up small objects – papers, cigarettes, a notebook. The mounting tension in the pit of Jack's stomach drove him away from the kitchen table, with a muttered apology, and up into the still-air privacy of his bedroom. He sat tensely on the edge of the bed, listening for the sound of the Lincoln crackling down the driveway.

When it finally came he went out on the landing and part way down the stairs. He stood there in the big house's dark brown silence, hovering, feeling like a pike meditatively selecting its level in dim waters. *Nine years*, he thought. *I'll die. I'll touch her, and I'll die.*

He went the rest of the way down, unable to prevent himself moving stealthily, and into the kitchen. Kate was standing near the window, washing apples. She did not look around, but went on dousing the pale green fruit with cold water. The simple domestic action struck Breton as being somehow incongruous.

'Kate,' he said. 'Why are you doing that?'

'Insecticides.' She still refused to turn her head. 'I always wash the apples.'

'I see. You've got to do it this morning? It's urgent, is it?'

'I want to put them away in the fridge.'

'But there's no hurry, is there?'

'No.' She sounded contrite, as though he had forced her to admit something shameful.

Breton felt guilty – he was really putting her through it. 'Did you ever notice the way fruit looks so much brighter and more colourful when it's submerged in water?'

'No.'

'It does. Nobody knows why. *Kate!*'

She turned to face him and he caught her hands. They were wet and cold, stirring ghastly memories far back in his mind. He kissed the chilled fingers, making his own private penance.

'Don't do that.' She tried to pull her hands away, but he tightened his grip.

'Kate,' he said urgently. 'I lost you nine years ago – but you lost something, too. John doesn't love you, and I do. It's as simple as that.'

'It isn't safe to make snap judgements about John.'

'For me it's safe. But just look at the facts – he went off to work this morning as if nothing had happened. Leaving us alone. Do you think I'd leave you alone with a declared rival? I'd . . .' Breton left the sentence unfinished. He had been going to say he would kill his rival first.

'That was John acting hurt. He tries mental judo, you know. If you push, he pulls. If you pull, he pushes.'

Kate was speaking quickly, in desperation, as Breton drew her to him. He slid his fingers gently up the fluted back of her neck, through the hair and gripped her head, turning her face to him. She resisted for a few seconds, then – all at once – came to him with mouth wide open. Breton kept his eyes open during that first kiss, trying to imprint the moment on his mind, to raise it beyond time itself.

Later, as they lay in the parchment-coloured light of the shuttered bedroom, Breton stared at the ceiling in wonderment. *So this*, he thought, *is sanity*. He let his brain absorb the sensations of relaxed well-being that were flooding in from every part of his body. In this mood, everything connected with the process of being alive was good. He could have got immense pleasure from a thousand simple things that had been forgotten somewhere along the way – climbing a hill, drinking beer, chopping wood, writing a poem.

He put his hand on the cool skin of Kate's thigh. 'How do you feel?'

'All right.' Her voice was sleepy, remote.

Breton nodded, looking at the room through his brand new eyes. The baffled sunlight had a yellowed, Mediterranean quality about it, restful yet absolutely clear. And it revealed no flaws in his Time B universe. A strangely relevant fragment from an old poem drifted into his mind.

The painted scenaries recall
Such toil as Canaletto spent
To give each brick upon each wall
Its due partition of cement.

He raised himself on one elbow and looked down at Kate. 'My name should have been Canaletto,' he said.

She stared up at him, half-smiling, then turned her face away and he knew she was thinking about John. Breton sank down on his pillow, absentmindedly sliding a finger beneath the strap of his watch to touch the hidden lump of the chronomotor module buried beneath his skin. John Breton was the one flaw in the Time B universe.

But that state of affairs was strictly temporary.

SEVEN

JAKE LARMOUR STARED wearily through the curved viewscreen of his crawler at the flat, monotonous surface of the Moon. He kept the vehicle's motors running at maximum revolutions, but the western rim of the Sea of Tranquillity, towards which he had been driving for the past two hours, seemed as far away as ever. At intervals he yawned widely, and between times whistled a thin, sad tune. Jake Larmour was bored.

Back in Pine Ridge, Wisconsin, the idea of being a radar maintenance man on the Moon had seemed glamorous and exciting. Now, after three months of patrolling the line towers, he had reached the stage of crossing off the days on a calendar hand-drawn for that express purpose. He had known in advance that the Moon was dead, but what he had not anticipated was the way in which his own spirit would quail in the face of such complete and utter absence of life.

If only, he thought for the thousandth time on that trip, if only something would *move* out there.

He was leaning back in an extravagant yawn, arms stretching as far as possible in the crawler's cockpit, when something flickered and vanished on the surface of the crater bed about a hundred yards ahead of him. Larmour instinctively hit the brake and the vehicle whined to a stop. He sat upright in his seat, scanning the ground beyond the viewscreen, wondering if his imagination was beginning to act up on him. Several elongated seconds dragged by while the lunar landscape waited complacently for eternity. Larmour's hand was moving towards the throttle levers when he saw the movement again, off to the left, and a little closer.

He swallowed hard. His eyes had focused more quickly this time and he had made out a fluffy grey object – about the size of a football – which had popped up above ground level for an instant before vanishing downwards. As he watched, the phenomenon was repeated three more times, always in a different place.

'Well, I'll be damned,' he said aloud. 'If I've discovered Moon gophers I'll be famous.'

Trembling a little, he reached for the radio button, then remembered there was too much of the Moon's humped back between him and Base Three to allow contact. Beyond the screen a fluffy ball peeked up impudently and disappeared. Larmour hesitated for only a second before he disconnected his relief tube, sealed up his pressure suit and began making all the arrangements necessary for a human being to observe before setting foot on the Moon. A few minutes later, suppressing a sense of unreality, he left the crawler and began moving uncertainly towards where he had seen the last flurry of movement. As he walked he kept his eyes open for the lunar equivalent of gopher holes, but the blanket of eons-old dust was smooth except for the untidy sutures of his own footprints.

Abruptly, several of the fluffy balls sprang up within a radius of fifty paces, making him snatch for breath. Summoning his presence of mind, he kept his gaze fixed on the spot where the nearest materialization had taken place. Larmour reached the place, labouring with his inexpert low-gravity shuffle, and his gingery brows knit together as he saw there was no hole which could possibly contain the furtive grey entity he was seeking.

He knelt down to alter the direction of the light rays reflecting from the dust, and thought he could discern a shallow, dish-shaped depression with a minute dimple in the centre. Becoming more and more puzzled, Larmour gently scooped the dust away with his hands until he had exposed the surface of the rock three inches below. There was a neat circular hole of about an inch diameter, looking as though it had been put there with a masonry drill. He pushed one finger into the hole, then jerked it out again as heat seared through the insulation of his glove. The surrounding rock was practically red hot.

Larmour sat back on his heels and stared at the black circle in perplexity. His mind was wrestling unsuccessfully with the problem it represented, when another grey ball appeared momentarily only a few feet away. This time he felt the ground tremors, and then suddenly he had the answer – the hideous, deadly answer.

On the Moon – with no air to buoy up its separate particles – a cloud of dust remains small and compact, and vanishes back into the ground almost as quickly as the eye can follow. And the only thing which would kick up such a cloud, human agencies excepted, was a meteor impact!

Larmour had left the safety of his vehicle and was walking about unprotected amid a meteor shower of unprecedented intensity, a hail of bullets fired a billion blind years earlier. Groaning at his own stupidity and lack of experience, he stood up and ran with ballooning Moon-steps towards the waiting crawler.

An obsolescent, four-engined aircraft was patiently clawing its way across the night skies of Northern Greenland. Inside its drumming, cylindrical belly, Denis Soderman carefully tended his banks of recording equipment, occasionally adjusting verniers, keeping the research plane's inhuman and far-reaching senses at their keenest. He worked with the abstracted efficiency of a man who knows his job is important but who believes he was cut out for higher things.

Some distance forward of Soderman's station, the senior – Dr Cosgrove – sat at a makeshift desk, running grey paper tape through his hands like a tailor measuring cloth. His still-young face looked old and tired in the clinical light from the overhead tube.

'We don't need to wait for a computer to process this lot, Denis,' Cosgrove said. 'The solar corpuscular streams are obviously boosted way beyond normal. I've never seen readings like this, even with freak sunspot activity. The Van Allen belt must be soaking the stuff up like a sponge, and with those reports of fluctuations in the solar constant we got today from M I T, it looks . . .'

Denis Soderman stopped listening. He was adept at shutting out the older man's ruminative voice, but this time it was more than a mere defence mechanism against the effects of unbridled pedantry. Something had happened to the aircraft. Seated far back from the machine's centre of gravity, Soderman had experienced a subtle, queasy corkscrewing motion. It had lasted perhaps half a second, but Soderman was a talented amateur pilot and had found something disturbing in the idea of a hundred-ton aircraft flicking its tail like a salmon. Emulating his electronic charges, he spread the network of his senses as wide as possible. For a few seconds he picked up nothing but the normal sensations of flight, then it happened again – a momentary lift and twist which made his stomach contract in alarm.

'They're having trouble up front,' he said. 'I don't like the way this old bus is flying.'

Cosgrove looked up from his perforated streamers. 'I didn't feel anything.' His voice registered disapproval of Soderman's lack of concentration on the job at hand.

'Listen, doctor. I'm way out on a limb here in the tail and I can *feel*—'

He broke off as the aircraft suddenly lurched sideways, shuddered, righted itself and became ominously quiet as all four engines cut out at the same time. Soderman, who had been lifted out of his seat and smashed against his instrument arrays, struggled to his feet and ran forward past Dr Cosgrove. There was a noticeable slope in the gangway, showing that the aircraft was now flying in a pronounced nose-down attitude. A grey-faced second officer collided with him in the doorway to the flight deck.

'Get up to the tail and get your backs against the lavatory bulkhead! We're going down!' The officer made no attempt to keep the panic out of his voice.

'Going down?' Soderman shouted. 'Going down where? There isn't a field within three hundred miles.'

'Are you telling *me* there's no field?'

Even in a crisis the airman was jealous of his superiority over ordinary mortals, resentful at having to discuss the affairs of his aerial domain with an outsider.

'We're doing everything we can to restart the engines, but Captain Isaacs isn't optimistic. It looks as though he'll have to try setting us down on the snow. Now will you go aft?'

'But it's *dark* out there! Nobody could put a ship down—'

'That's our problem, mister.' The officer pushed Soderman up the swaying gangway and turned back to the flight deck. Soderman's mouth was dry as he moved aft, following the stumbling figure of Dr Cosgrove.

They reached the conical tail-section and sat on the floor, backs braced against the cool metal of a major bulkhead. This far from the centre of gravity each control movement made by the pilot was felt as a great, wild swing which gave Soderman the conviction the final catastrophe had arrived. With no sound from the engines to mask it, the passage of the fuselage through the air was loud, variable, menacing – the gleeful voice of a sky which could feel an enemy's strength bleeding away.

Soderman tried to reconcile himself to the thought of dying

within a matter of minutes, knowing that no combination of luck, pilot's skill and structural integrity could enable the aircraft to survive contact with the earth. In daylight, or even in moonlight, it might have worked, but in pitch blackness there could be only one outcome to this rushing descent.

He clenched his teeth and vowed to go out with at least as much dignity as Dr Cosgrove seemed to have mustered – but, when the impact came, he screamed. His voice was lost in a prolonged metallic thunderclap, then the plane was airborne again in a crazy, slewing leap, culminating in another incredible blast of sound which was compounded by the clattering of moveable objects bounding the length of the fuselage. The nightmare seemed to last for an eternity, during which all the interior lights were extinguished, but it ended abruptly, and Soderman discovered he was still breathing – miraculously, impossibly alive.

A few minutes later he was standing at an emergency door peering into the night sky at the glowing face of his saviour.

Striated curtains of red and green light shimmered and danced from horizon to horizon, illuminating the snowscape below with an eerie, theatrical brilliance. It was an auroral display of supernatural intensity.

'This illustrates what I was saying about the Van Allen belt being overloaded,' Dr Cosgrove commented emotionlessly behind Soderman. 'The solar corpuscular stream is washing the upper atmosphere with charged particles which are draining into the magnetic poles. Their display, to which it seems we owe our lives, is only one facet of . . .'

But Soderman had stopped listening – he was too busy with the pleasurable business of simply being alive.

Dr Fergus B. Raphael sat quietly at the wheel of his car, staring across the oil-dappled concrete of the university parking lot.

He was seriously contemplating driving away towards the ocean and never being heard of in academic circles again. There had been a time when he had tackled his work with supreme enthusiasm, undeterred by the realization that – in the very nature of things – he would never achieve the rewards which were possible for workers in other fields. But the years had taken their toll, the years of living on the wrong side of the scientific tracks, and now he was tired.

He put aside the daily pretence that he was free to drive away from his obsession, and got out of the car. The sky was overcast and chestnut leaves were scuttling noisily before a cold, searching wind. Raphael turned up his coat collar and walked towards the unremarkable architecture of the university. It looked like being yet another very ordinary day.

Half an hour later he had set up the first experiment of the morning. The volunteer was Joe Washburn, a young Negro student who had shown flashes of promise in a previous series of tests.

Raphael raised a microphone to his lips. 'All set, Joe?'

Washburn nodded and waved to Raphael through the window of his soundproof booth. Raphael moved a switch and checked with his assistant, Jean Ard, who was sitting in a similar booth at the opposite side of the laboratory. She gave him an exaggeratedly cheerful wave, which Raphael took as an indication that she too was feeling depressed. He started the recording machine, then leaned back in his chair, unwrapping a cigar, and watched the visual monitors with dutiful eyes.

Not for the first time, he thought: *how long does this farce have to go on? How much proof do I need that mind-to-mind communication is impossible?*

Jean Ard keyed in her first symbol and a triangle appeared on her monitor. Her face was impassive behind the thick glass of the booth and Raphael wondered if she always tried to concentrate and project, or if she ever just sat there, pushed buttons and thought about her evening date. A few minutes later Washburn's monitor lit up – triangle. Raphael ignored his cigar and waited, wondering how soon he could break off and go for coffee. A square appeared on Jean's monitor, followed by a square on Washburn's. She tried a triangle again, and Washburn matched her. Then a circle and a star, and Washburn registered a circle and a star. In spite of himself,

Raphael's pulse began to quicken and he felt a recurrence of the old nervous fever which might have made him a chronic gambler had he not found a way to sublimate it in research. He watched closely as Jean continued keying in at random the five abstract symbols they used in the telepathy experiments. Eight minutes later she had gone through a complete test sample of fifty projections.

And Joe Washburn's score was exactly fifty.

Raphael stubbed out his cigar with a shaking hand. He felt deathly cold as he raised the microphone, but he kept his voice as flat as possible to avoid injecting even the minutest disturbance into the experiment.

'That was all right for a warm-up, Jean and Joe. Let's run through another set.' They both nodded. He moved a switch and spoke to Jean only. 'I'd like you to use both the abstract and the related symbols this time.'

He hunched over the console and watched the monitors with the eyes of a man playing Russian roulette. The addition of the five meaningful symbols – tree, automobile, dog, chair, man – brought the range up to ten, and made a freak run of success that much more difficult.

Washburn made one mistake in the next series of fifty, and no errors at all in the following three sets. Raphael decided to introduce the demons of emotion and self-consciousness.

'Listen, you two,' he said thickly. 'I don't know how you're doing it, but you've been scoring virtually one hundred per cent since this experiment started, and I don't have to tell you what that means. Now let's keep blasting away at this thing till we see how far it's going to go.'

Washburn made four mistakes in the next set, two in the following set, and none in the five further tests which Raphael put him through before switching off the recording equipment. Both Jean and Washburn had to examine the print-out for themselves before they accepted that the whole affair had not been a trick devised by Raphael to introduce a new experimental factor. When the truth had sunk in they stared at each other with cautious, wondering eyes.

'I think it'd be a good idea if we had some coffee now, Jean,' Raphael said. 'This needs some thinking about.'

While Jean was fixing coffee, Joe Washburn wandered around the laboratory grinning, shaking his head and driving his fist into the palm of his left hand. Raphael lit another cigar and put it out almost immediately, realizing he would have to tell somebody about what had happened. He went to the phone and was on the point of lifting it when it rang.

'A long-distance call for you, Dr Raphael,' the university operator said. 'It's Professor Morrison calling from Cleveland.'

'Thank you,' Raphael said dully, shocked at the coincidence. He had been going to call Morrison, who was his closest friend among the handful of men still working in the unfashionable field of extra-sensory perception. Somehow, he had a prescient awareness of why Morrison was calling, and the feeling was confirmed when he heard the other man's excited tones.

'Hello, Fergus? Thank God I got hold of you – I had to get this off my chest to somebody before I exploded. You'll never guess what's been happening here.'

'I will,' Raphael said.

'Try it then.'

'You've begun getting hundred-per-cent successes in telepathy experiments.'

Morrison's gasp of surprise was clearly audible. 'That's right. How did you know?'

'Perhaps,' Raphael said sombrely, 'I'm telepathic too.'

EIGHT

A FULL DAY had passed before Jack Breton's consternation over the fragment of poetry began to abate.

He had questioned Kate about it as closely as he dared and, when he learned how it had been written, pretended a sympathetic interest in automatic writing. Kate had seemed pleased and flattered at his support, and had explained in detail everything she knew about Miriam Palfrey's powers.

Becoming more and more uneasy, Breton had examined hundreds of samples of the automatic writing and learned that the piece of verse was the only thing of its kind Miriam had ever produced. Furthermore, she had done it within hours of his arrival in the Time B world – which would hardly be a coincidence. The only answer his mind could produce, no matter how he juggled the facts, was telepathy – and the last thing he wanted was somebody reading his mind.

On the following morning his guess, wild as it had seemed, was confirmed in an unexpected manner. The apparent breakdown in John Breton's relationship with Kate had accelerated visibly since Jack's arrival. He had become more withdrawn, more caustic when he did speak of her, obviously in the throes of assessing his whole life. And, as if to assert his claim to an independent existence in his own universe, he constantly patrolled the house with a radio tucked in the crook of his arm, turning it to full volume at every news broadcast.

The newscasts he overheard told one part of Jack Breton's mind that some very unusual events were taking place, but he was too deeply involved in working out his own personal destiny to pay much attention to stories of scientific curiosities. Had he not been weighing up his plans in the light of the fact that Miriam Palfrey appeared to have snatched something right out of his mind, he would not have absorbed the news that telepathy experiments in several universities had suddenly begun to yield dramatic results. The information served to demote Miriam from the status of an inexplicable menace to that of the other background phenomena.

Strangely, Jack Breton found no deterioration in his relationship with his other self. The big house was filled with almost-tangible currents of emotion as John and Kate manoeuvred endlessly, each waiting for the other to break the stasis which had descended on them. But at odd moments Jack discovered himself in a calm backwater in which he and John could talk like twin brothers who had not met in a long time. He also discovered, and was mildly surprised, that John's memory of their common boyhood was much more detailed and complete than his own. Several times he argued with John about the authenticity of some detail until the relevant compartment of his mind seemed to open suddenly, admitting the vari-coloured stains of memory, and he realized John had been right.

A tentative explanation reached by Jack was that memories were reinforced by repetition of the act of recall – and, at some time during the past nine years, John Breton had begun to live in the past. Some dissatisfaction with the shape of his life in the Time B world had led him to draw on the stored comforts of a bygone era.

Even in the short time he had been in the house Jack had noticed John's obsessive interest in old movies, the way in which he invariably compared people to the old-time actors and actresses. Photographs of Thirties-style cars with their tiny vertical windshields were hung around the basement workshop. ('I'd love to drive one of those myopic old things,' John had said. 'Can't you *smell* the dust in those big cloth-covered seats?') And when he had lifted himself clear of the past, he avoided the human realities of the present, sinking his mind into the engineering and commercial disciplines of running the Breton Consultancy.

Jack Breton received the up-to-date details of the business gratefully – he was going to need all available information when the time came for him to take over. It also gave him the opportunity to establish one fact which was vital to his plan . . .

'Gravimetric surveying has become impossible of course,' John was saying after lunch. 'The Bureau of Standards came right out and said it this morning – the force of gravity is decreasing. It always did fluctuate, and I'm willing to bet we're simply on the downward slope of a more massive variation than usual, but all the same, it's funny the news broadcasts don't make more of it. I mean, there's nothing more basic than gravity. Perhaps there's been a clamp-down of some kind.'

'I doubt it,' Jack said absently, thinking of Kate upstairs

in the same house, perhaps in the bedroom adjusting her plumage.

'At least gravimeters are all right. Carl and I were worried. Did you have him in your set-up? Carl Tougher?'

'Yes. Hetty and he took over the business.' Kate might be moving naked through the guilty afternoon twilight of closed blinds.

'It wouldn't have mattered too much about the gravimeters, luckily. There was a time when a gravimeter, a theodolite and a couple of ex-Army Dumpy levels were just about all the capital equipment I had. That was before I started accepting bore-hole contracts and some large-bore work.'

Jack's interest was suddenly aroused. 'How about these new non-physical drills? The matter disrupter gadgets? Do you use those?'

'Got three of them,' John replied warmly. 'We use them for all the large-bore drilling. Carl doesn't like them because they don't have a coring facility, but they're fast and clean. You can sink a two-foot hole through any kind of strata, and it all comes up as micro-dust.'

'I've never seen one in action,' Jack said with deliberate wistfulness. 'Are there any sites close to town?'

'The nearest is about twenty miles north of here on the main route to Silverstream.' John sounded doubtful. 'I don't see how you could get out there, though. People are going to start wondering if they see two of us walking around.'

'But that situation's going to be corrected soon.'

'Is it?' John Breton was instantly suspicious, and Jack wondered if he had any inkling of the fate planned for him.

'Of course,' he said quickly. 'You and Kate are bound to reach a decision any time now. In fact, I don't see what's taking you so long. Why don't you admit that you're sick to death of each other, and get it over with?'

'Has Kate said anything to you?'

'No,' Jack replied cautiously, not wanting to precipitate a crisis before he was completely ready to handle it.

'Well – anytime she works up the nerve to say what she's thinking, I'll be ready to hear her out.' A look of schoolboyish truculence passed over John's square face, and Jack realized his own instincts had been right all along. No man would ever willingly give up a prize like Kate. The only solution to the triangle problem lay in two pieces of machinery – the pistol hidden upstairs in his room, and the matter disrupter drill along the Silverstream highway.

'Is it important for you to get Kate to make the first move?'

'If you don't analyse me, I won't analyse you,' John said significantly.

Jack smiled at him, calmly. The reference to analysis made him think of John's body converted to micro-dust, completely anonymous, defying any kind of investigation.

When John had returned to the office, Jack waited hungrily for Kate to come downstairs to him, but she appeared dressed in a tweed suit with tied belt and a high fur collar.

'Going out?' He tried to mask his disappointment.

'Shopping,' she said in a business-like voice which hurt him in some obscure fashion.

'Don't go.'

'But we still have to eat.' Her voice carried what he recognized as a trace of antagonism, and he suddenly realized she had been virtually avoiding him since their single physical encounter. The idea that she might be feeling guilt – and associating him with it – filled Breton with an unreasoning panic.

'John's talking about pulling out.' He was unable to prevent himself blurting the lie like a love-sick adolescent, in spite of his awareness of the need to prepare her mind for John's disappearance more carefully than he had ever done anything in his entire life. Kate hesitated between him and the door. The down on her cheekbones caught the light like frost, and he seemed to see the mortuary drawer supporting her on its efficient cantilever. He became afraid.

'John's entitled to leave if he wants,' she said finally, and went out. A minute later he heard her MG booming in the garage. He waited at the window to see her go by, but the car was fitted with its hardtop and Kate's face was an impersonal blur behind the chiselled sky-fragments of the windows.

Breton turned away from the window, suddenly filled with a sense of outrage. Both his creations – the people he had brought into being as surely as if he had stalked the Earth amid Biblical lightnings, putting breath into inert clay – had lived independently of him for nine years. Now, in spite of what they had learned, they were insisting on pursuing their courses, ignoring him when necessary, leaving him alone in a house where he hated to be alone. Breton moved with clenched fists through the silences of the empty rooms. He had been prepared to wait a week, but things had changed and were still doing so. It would be necessary to act more quickly, more decisively.

From a rear window he glimpsed the silvery dome of the observatory beyond the beech trees, and felt a grudging curiosity about its construction. Right from the moment of his arrival there had been a tacit, instinctive agreement that nobody outside the house should get any clue about the existence of the two Bretons – so he could not justify going outside. But the rear garden was well shielded from the neighbouring houses, and it would take him only a few seconds to reach the observatory and get inside.

He went down into the kitchen, peered through the curtained door and went out on to the roofed patio. The lemon-tinted sunlight of an October afternoon streamed through the trees in slowly merging beams, and from the distance came the patient, regular sound of a lawn mower. Breton walked towards the observatory.

'Ho there! Not working today?'

Breton spun as the voice came from behind him. The speaker was a tall, fit-looking man of about forty who had just come around the side of the house. He was dressed in neat sports clothes, worn the way other men wear business suits, and his tightly-waved hair was greyed at the temples. His face was broad and sun-burned, with a tiny nose which made scarcely any division between widely-spaced blue eyes.

Breton experienced a thrill of almost superstitious dread

as he recognized Lieutenant Convery – the man who, in another time-stream, had come to tell him of Kate's death – but he remained in perfect control of his reactions.

'Not today,' he said, smiling. 'A man has to relax every now and then.'

'I didn't know you felt that way, John.'

'But I do, I do – I don't make a habit of it, that's all.' Breton noticed the other man's use of his Christian name, and tried unsuccessfully to think of Convery's. This is incredible, he thought. How can a man *have* such bad luck?

Convery smiled, showing very white teeth made even more brilliant in places by slight fluoride mottling. 'I'm glad to hear you don't work all the time, John – it makes me feel less of a slob.'

John again, Breton thought. I can't call him Lieutenant if we're on first-name terms. 'Well, what brings you out this way?'

'Nothing much – a couple of routine calls in the area.' Convery reached into his pocket. 'So I brought this.' He brought out a brown pebble-like object and handed it to Breton.

'Oh, yes.' Breton inspected the object, noting its segmented, spiral construction. 'Oh, yes?'

'Yeah. My boy got it from another kid at school. I told him I'd get you to . . .' He let his voice trail away, and stood waiting.

Breton stared down at the coiled stone, mind racing desperately. He remembered Kate saying that Convery sometimes called to drink coffee with John and talk about fossils. Presumably this was because John had some professional knowledge of geology. Did it include fossils? He tried to send his mind back more than nine years to the time when he too had been interested in the rock-embalmed time travellers.

'This is a reasonably fair ammonite,' he said, praying that Convery merely wanted a simple identification.

Convery nodded. 'Age?'

'About two hundred and fifty million years – hard to say for sure without knowing where it was found.'

'Thanks.' Convery took the fossil back and dropped it in his pocket. His intelligent blue eyes flickered momentarily and Breton suddenly knew that his relationship with the other Breton was a complex and uneasy thing. 'Say, John?'

'Uh-huh?' Why, Breton wondered, did he insist on using the first name so much?

'You're losing some weight, aren't you?'

'It's nice of you to notice it. A fellow can get discouraged if he goes on dieting for weeks without any obvious result.'

'I'd say you've lost seven or eight pounds.'

'That's about right – and I really feel better for it.'

'I think you looked better the way you were, John,' Convery said thoughtfully. 'You look tired.'

'I am tired – that's why I took the afternoon off.' Breton laughed, and Convery joined in.

Breton remembered the coffee. 'Do you feel like risking a cup of coffee brewed with my own hand? Kate's out shopping.'

'Where's Mrs Fitz?'

Breton's mind went numb, then he recalled that Mrs Fitz was the cook-housekeeper. 'We gave her a few days off,' he said easily. 'She has to rest too, you know.'

'I guess I'll just have to risk your coffee then, John.'

Convery pushed open the kitchen door and ushered Breton inside. While Breton was preparing the coffee he considered the problem of the fact that they were supposed to know each other's preferences about cream and sugar, and circumvented it by setting both on the kitchen table in advance. He found the familiar domestic activity relaxing, realizing he had been needlessly alarmed over Convery's visit. Kate had said the policeman sometimes dropped by to talk about fossils and drink coffee – and that was exactly what was happening. Even if Kate were to return right then there would be nothing to arouse Convery's curiosity, and John Breton was not expected for at least three hours.

Breton took his coffee black and so hot that flat grey films of vapour crazed its surface. Convery took cream but no sugar, and sipped it with evident appreciation. While he drank he raised the subject of the meteor bombardments which were turning the night skies into firework displays. Pleased at finding the conversation turning to something which placed him on an equal footing with any other inhabitant of the Time B universe, Breton discussed the meteors willingly.

'Back to work,' Convery said when he had finished his second cup. 'Us minions of the law aren't supposed to laze around like this.' He stood up and carried his cup and saucer over to the sink unit.

'That's life,' Breton said uninspiredly.

He said goodbye to Convery in the patio and went back into the house, filled with a heady sense of satisfaction. There was now nothing to stop him going ahead with his plan to step into John Breton's shoes. The one point about which he had been uncertain was his ability to meet people who knew John and be with them for extended periods without arousing suspicions or, at least, curiosity. But he had carried off the encounter with Lieutenant Convery well, extremely well, and could see that there was nothing to be gained by delaying things any further – especially since Kate's emotional reactions were showing signs of becoming complicated.

Jack Breton went upstairs to the guest bedroom, took the pistol from its hiding place deep in a closet, and laid the cool, oily metal against his lips.

NINE

WHEN LIEUTENANT BLAIZE CONVERY was a boy of four, his mother once told him that deaf-and-dumb people usually learned 'to talk with their hands'.

He decided then and there that this would be a useful and fascinating accomplishment, even for a person who had all his faculties. For the next three years the infant Convery devoted some time every day to learning the secret, sitting alone in his room, staring at his right hand while putting it through every conceivable contortion, hoping to discover the magical combination of flexures and tensions which would cause a voice to issue from his palm. When he finally found out, through another chance remark, that his mother had been referring to sign language he abandoned his quest immediately and without regrets. He had learned the truth, and was satisfied.

When Lieutenant Blaize Convery was a boy of seven, his father had shown him a diagram consisting of a square, nested inside a circle, with straight lines connecting the corners laterally. It was possible, his father had said, to reproduce that diagram without lifting his pencil or going over any line twice. Convery worked on the puzzle at odd moments for six years.

After the first month he was virtually certain it was impossible – but his father, who had died in the meantime, had claimed he had seen it done – so he kept on gnawing at the problem. Then he had chanced on a magazine biography of the eighteenth-century Swiss mathematician Leonard Euler, founder of topography. The article mentioned Euler's solution of the problem of the seven bridges of Königsberg, proving it was possible to cross all of them without crossing any twice. It also mentioned, incidentally, that the same proof provided a way to check on the solvability of diagram puzzles – count the number of lines entering each node of the diagram, and if more than two of them have an odd number, you cannot draw it without going over a line or lifting your pencil.

Again, he had closed a mental file, satisfied at having reached a firm conclusion one way or the other, and the pattern of thinking that was to make him a very special kind of policeman was already sharpening into focus.

He had gone into the force almost automatically, but – in spite of excellent academic qualifications – had not made his expected progress through the ranks. A good police executive learns to live with the statistics of his profession. He accepts the fact that while some crimes are solvable most are not, and channels his energies accordingly; optimizing gains, cutting losses.

But Blaize Convery was known in the force as a 'sticker' –

a man who was constitutionally incapable of letting go a problem once he had got his teeth into it. His seniors and fellow detectives respected his personal record of successes, but it was a standing joke in the area that the chief of the records bureau had resorted to making secret raids on Convery's desk to get back sizeable sections of his filing system.

Convery understood his own idiosyncrasies, and knew how they were affecting his career. He frequently resolved to alter his approach to the job, often managing to conform for weeks on end, but just as it was beginning to look as though he had won his subconscious would throw up a new slant on a three-year-old investigation, and an icy, egotistical joy would start churning his stomach. This moment, Convery knew, was the crunch: his own private version of the experience which made other men great religious leaders, immortal artists, or short-lived combat heroes. He had never resisted its mystical blandishments, and had never been disappointed in the rewards, or lack of them.

And as he drove away from the Breton house, through tree-guarded avenues, Convery could feel that arctic elation stalking the pathways of his nervous system.

He guided his elderly but well-maintained Plymouth past green lawns, reviewing the Breton-Spiedel affair, reaching nine years into the receding past. The case was unique in his memory, not for the fact that he had failed to crack it – there had been many failures in his career – but because he had been so monumentally wrong. Convery had been in the station when Kate Breton was brought in, and he had got most of the story from her in those first stunned minutes while a policewoman was washing flecks of human brain tissue from her hair.

Compressed to its essentials, her story was that she and her husband had fought on the way to a party. She had gone on alone on foot, foolishly taking a shortcut through the park, and had been attacked. A man had appeared from nowhere, put a bullet through the attacker's head, and vanished again into the night. Kate Breton had run blindly until she was on the point of collapse.

Working on those bare facts, Convery had reached two possible explanations. He had begun by immediately dismissing the idea that it had all happened by chance, that a mysterious stranger had just happened to be walking in the park at the right moment, carrying a high-powered rifle. This left the possibility that the marksman was someone who knew the attacker and suspected him of being a psychotic killer, who had trailed him until he had positive proof, and then carried out a summary execution. It was a theory which Convery had rejected instinctively, although he would check it out as a matter of course.

He had found his mind drawn into a vortex centred on Kate Breton's husband. Suppose the car breakdown and the subsequent fight had been planned? Suppose Kate Breton's husband had wanted to get rid of her and had brought a gun in the trunk of his car? He could have followed her to the park, been about to shoot when the attack occurred, and on the spur of the moment fired at the attacker.

The second theory had holes in it, but Convery was experienced at plugging holes. He had begun by asking Kate Breton if she had any idea who did the shooting. Still in a state of shock, she had shaken her head – but Convery had seen the curve of her lower lip deepen as she subvocalized a word, a name beginning with J.

And when he had gone to the Breton house, armed with the description provided by the teenagers who had seen the shooting ... And when he had read the guilt in Breton's eyes, he had *known* that here was his killer ...

The discovery that Breton could not be touched had wounded Convery in some obscure way he could hardly understand. He had spent weeks trying to shake the alibi given to Breton by the neighbours who had noticed him standing at his front window; and he had made himself unpopular with the forensic staff by insisting they could have been wrong about the rifle not being fired. Convery had even experimented with an old deer rifle – firing it, cleaning it with various solutions and spraying it with dust. But in the end he had acknowledged that Breton, the man who had charged the very air with his guilt, could not be touched.

For any other cop, that would have been the time to close the file and move on to something more promising – but Convery's demon was perched firmly on his shoulder, whispering its heady promises of fulfilment. And as he drove homewards he could hear its voice suddenly grown strong again. There had been times during the past nine years when his visits to the Breton house had seemed utterly pointless, acts of monomania, but today he had smelled the fear and the guilt . . .

Convery swung the Plymouth on to the short concrete walk outside his own house, narrowly missing a tricycle belonging to his youngest son. He got out of the car and as he was closing the door detected a faint squeak from one of the hinges. After swinging the door several more times to satisfy himself about the location of the tiny sound, he went into the garage, brought out an oilcan and lubricated the hinges on all four doors. He put the can back in its own appointed place then went through the inner door, through the utilities room, and into the kitchen.

'You're late, darling.' His wife, Gina, was standing at a table which was covered with baking requisites. Her forearms were streaked with flour and the warm air of the kitchen was filled with the nostalgic odour of mince pies.

'Sorry,' Convery said. 'I got held back.' He patted his wife on the rump, absentmindedly lifted a piece of candied peel and began to nibble at it.

'Blaize?'

'What is it, honey?'

'Were you over at the Breton house again?'

Convery stopped chewing. 'What makes you ask?'

'Tim said you'd been into his fossil collection again. He said his ammonite was missing.'

'Hey!' Convery laughed. 'I thought I was the detective in this house.'

'But were you there?'

'Well, I did stop by for a few minutes.'

'Oh, Blaize – what must those people think?' Gina Convery's face showed her concern.

'Why should they think anything? It was just a friendly call.'

'People are never friendly with a detective who has investigated them in a murder case. Specially people with their sort of money.'

'There's no need to get all tensed up over it, honey – John Breton and I get along well together.'

'I can imagine,' Gina said as Convery went through into the lounge. He sat down, picked up a magazine and turned the pages unseeingly. Something very strange had happened in the Breton household nine years earlier, and today had been like a trip back through time to that focus of stress. As well as being thinner, Breton had looked older – yet, in an indefinable way, he had seemed younger, less experienced, less sure of himself, emitting a different aura. *I'm going crazy*, Convery thought. *Auras aren't evidence – not unless this telepathy thing that's been in the news is really beginning to spread*. He leafed through the magazine, picked up another, then threw it down in disgust.

'Gina,' he called. 'What time do we eat?'

'About five – soon enough for you?'

'That's fine. I've got to go out again.'

A second later Convery found himself sitting in the middle of a kind of floury explosion as his wife burst into the room and began waving her fist under his nose.

'Blaize Convery,' she whispered ferociously. 'You leave this house over my dead body.'

Convery looked up into her pink, determined face in mild surprise. 'I don't get it.'

'Tim's having his birthday party – why do you think I'm baking these cookies?'

'But his birthday isn't till next week,' Convery protested.

'I know, but Kenneth's birthday was *last* week, and they always have their party halfway between.' Gina stared at him accusingly. 'You should know that by this time.'

'I do know it, honey. I'd forgotten, that's all. Look, they won't mind if I miss it just this once ...'

'Just this once! You've missed it the past two years, and you aren't leaving this house tonight.'

'But I've got a job to do.'

'Not tonight.'

Convery looked into his wife's eyes and what he saw there made him give in, smiling in order to retrieve as much as possible of his dignity. When she had left the room he shrugged theatrically for the benefit of nobody but himself and picked up his magazine. John Breton had kept for nine years – he could wait a little longer.

TEN

WHEN THE PHONE rang, splintering the silence of the house, Breton hurried to it, but paused uncertainly with his fingers on the cool plastic curvature of the handset.

Two hours alone in the shadowed stillness of the afternoon had filled him with vague forebodings, which had alternated with moods of chest-pounding triumph. It was exactly the sort of day on which at one time he could have expected any moment to see the furtive, fugitive glimmering in his sight preceding a full-scale attack of hemicrania. But in the year since he'd had that first massive jump there had been scarcely any trips – the reservoir of nervous potential had been discharged, drained away. Now, with the phone trembling under his hand, there was nothing in his mind other than a sense of imminence, an awareness of life and death balancing on a knife-edge ...

He picked up the phone and waited without speaking.

'Hello.' The male voice on the wire was faintly Anglicized. 'Is that you, John?'

'Yes.' Breton spoke cautiously.

'I wasn't sure if you'd be there yet. I called the office and they said you'd left, but that was only five minutes ago, old boy – you must have been burning rubber on the way home.'

'I was moving.' Breton kept his voice relaxed. 'By the way – who is this?'

'It's Gordon, of course. Gordon Palfrey. Listen, old boy, I've got Kate with me. Miriam and I bumped into her in the Foodmart – she wants to speak to you.'

'All right.' With an effort Breton remembered that the Palfreys were the automatic writing enthusiasts who had captured Kate's interests. Miriam was the one who appeared to have some kind of telepathic faculty, and the thought of perhaps having to speak to her made him feel uneasy.

'Hello . . . John?' Kate sounded slightly breathless, and he knew from her hesitation over the phone that she knew who had really answered the call.

'What is it, Kate?'

'John, Miriam's been telling me the most fascinating things about her work. The results she's been getting in the last couple of days are just fantastic. I'm so excited for her.'

How, Breton thought, with a flicker of annoyance, *did Kate, my Kate, get herself mixed up with people like that?*

Aloud, he said, 'That sounds interesting. Is it what you called me about?'

'In a way – Miriam's giving a demonstration to a few close friends this evening and she's invited me. I'm so thrilled, John. You won't mind if I go straight there with them now, will you? You could look after yourself for one evening?'

Having Kate out of the house for the next few hours suited Breton's plans perfectly, yet he became angry at her almost religious attitude towards the Palfreys. Only the fear of sounding like the other Breton prevented him from protesting.

'Kate,' he said calmly. 'Are you avoiding me?'

'Of course not – it's just that I can't pass up this chance.'

'You love me?'

There was a pause. 'I didn't think you'd have any need to ask that.'

'All right.' Breton decided to begin positive action. 'But Kate, do you think it's wise to stay out this evening? I wasn't kidding about John, you know. He's in a mood in which he could pull up stakes tonight and vanish.'

'That's up to him. Would you object?'

'No – but I want you both to be sure about what you're doing.'

'I can't think about it,' Kate said, with the excitement suddenly gone from her voice. 'I just can't handle it.'

'Don't worry, darling.' Breton spoke softly. 'You go on and have fun. We'll work this out – somehow.'

He set the phone down and considered his next move. Gordon Palfrey had said John had already left the office, which meant he could arrive home at any minute. Breton sprinted up the stairs and removed the automatic pistol from its hiding place in the guest bedroom. Its metallic solidity dragged heavily in the side pocket of his jacket as he came out of the room. To make it look as though John Breton really had walked out of his marriage and career in disgust it would be necessary to get rid of the clothing and other effects he would be likely to take. *Money!* Jack Breton looked at his watch – the bank would be closed. He hesitated, wondering if Kate would notice anything suspicious if John supposedly took off into the blue without cash. It might not occur to her for a few days, or even weeks, but in the end it would begin to look strange.

On the other hand, she had never been a money-conscious person and would be unlikely to inquire too closely into the mechanics of any financial transaction John was supposed to have made. Jack decided to go to the bank first thing in the morning, as his other self, and arrange the transfer of a sizeable amount to a bank in Seattle. Later he could, if required, arrange to make withdrawals from the new account, to lend solidity to the fiction.

He took two expanding suitcases from a closet, filled them with clothes and brought them down into the hall. The pistol kept bumping against his hipbone. One part of his mind realized it was going to be difficult to use it on John Breton, but the rest of him was savagely aware that this was the culmination of nine years of agonized dedication, and there was no turning back. The essential point was that he had *created* John Breton's life, lent him nine years of existence for which there had never been any provision in the cosmic scheme, and now the time had come to foreclose on the loan. *I gave*, the thought came unbidden, *and I take away* . . .

Suddenly Breton felt deathly cold. He stood shivering in the hall, staring at himself in the long gold-tinted mirror, until – eons later – the deep whine of John Breton's Turbo-Lincoln disturbed the still brown air of the old house. A minute later John came in through the rear door and walked into the hall, still wearing his car-coat. His eyes narrowed as he saw the two suitcases.

'Where's Kate?' By tacit agreement, the two Bretons had dropped all the conventional formalities of greeting.

'She . . . she's having dinner with the Palfreys, and staying over there for the rest of the evening.' Jack found difficulty in forming the words. He was going to kill John within a matter of seconds, but the thought of seeing that familiar body torn open by bullets filled him with an unnerving timidity.

'I see.' John's eyes were watchful. 'What are you doing with my cases?'

Jack's fingers closed around the butt of the pistol. He shook his head, unable to speak.

'You don't look well,' John said. 'Are you all right?'

'I'm leaving,' Jack lied, struggling with the newly-made discovery that he would be unable to pull the trigger. 'I'll return your cases later. I took some clothes as well. Do you mind?'

'No, I don't mind.' Relief showed in John's eyes. 'But do you mean you're staying in this . . . time-stream?'

'Yes – as long as I know Kate's still alive somewhere, not too far away, that'll do me.'

'Oh!' There was a baffled expression on John Breton's square face, as though he had expected to hear something entirely different. 'Are you leaving right now? Do you want me to call you a taxi?'

Jack nodded. John shrugged and turned towards the telephone. The icy paralysis was dragging at Jack's muscles as he pulled the pistol out of his pocket. He stepped up close behind his other self and smashed the heavy butt into John's skull, just behind the ear. As John's knees buckled he hit him again and, in his uncoordinated numbness, stumbled and went down with him. He found himself sprawled on top of the other man, faces almost touching, watching in horror as John's eyes flickered open in pain-dulled consciousness.

'So it's like that,' John whispered in a semblance of drowsy satisfaction, like a child on the verge of sleep. His eyes closed but Jack Breton hit him again and again, using his fist, sobbing as he tried to destroy the image of his own guilt.

When sanity returned he rolled away from John and crouched beside the inert body, breathing heavily. He got to his feet, went up the shallow staircase to the bathroom and hunched over the washbasin. The metal of the taps was ice cold against his forehead, just as it had been when, as a young man making his first disastrous experiments with liquor, he had sprawled in the same attitude waiting for his system to cleanse itself. But this time relief was not to be purchased so easily.

Breton splashed his face with cold water and dried himself, taking special care over his knuckles, which were skinned and already beginning to exude clear fluid. He opened the bathroom cabinet in search of medical dressings and his attention was caught by a bottle of pale green triangles. They had the unmistakable generic look of sleeping tablets. Breton examined the label and confirmed his guess.

In the kitchen he filled a glass with water and carried it to the hall where John Breton was still sprawled on the mustard carpet. He raised John's head and began feeding him tablets. The task was more difficult than he had expected. The unconscious man's throat and mouth would fill up with water and an explosive cough would spew it and the tablets down on to his chest. Breton was sweating, and an unguessable amount of valuable time had gone by, before he had managed to get eight tablets down John's throat.

He threw the bottle aside, picked up the pistol, put it in

his pocket and dragged the body into the kitchen. A quick search of John's pockets provided Breton with a wallet full of identification he was going to need later in his dealings with the outside world, and a bunch of keys including those of the big Lincoln.

He went out to the car and drove it around to the back of the house then reversed so that the rear bumper was nuzzling the ivy-covered trellis of the patio. The air was warm from the afternoon sunshine and the distant lawn mower was still going its unconcerned way beyond the screens of trees and shrubbery. Breton opened the trunk of the car and went back into the kitchen. John was very still, as though already dead, and his face had a luminescent pallor. A single delta of blood extended from his nose across one cheek.

Breton dragged the body out of the house and manhandled it into the open trunk. While tucking the legs in he noticed that one of John's slip-on shoes was missing. He pulled down the lid of the trunk without locking it and went into the house. The shoe was lying just inside the doorway.

Breton picked it up and was hurrying back to the Lincoln when he walked straight into Lieutenant Convery.

'Sorry to disturb you again, John.' Convery's wide-set blue eyes were alert, dancing with a kind of malicious energy. 'I think I might've left something here.'

'I . . . I didn't notice anything sitting around.'

Breton heard the words issuing from his own mouth, and marvelled at his body's ability to continue with the intricacies of communication while the mind nominally in control was reeling with shock. What was Convery *doing* here? This was the second time in one day that he had materialized on the patio at the worst possible moment.

'It's the fossil. My boy's fossil – I didn't have it when I got home.' Convery's smile was almost derisive, as if he was challenging Breton to exercise his prerogative and throw an interfering cop off his property. 'You've no idea of the trouble I got into at home.'

'Well, I don't think it's here. I'm sure I would have noticed – it isn't the sort of thing you would overlook.'

'That's right,' Convery said carelessly. 'I guess I left it somewhere else.'

All this was no coincidence, Breton realized sadly. Convery was dangerous – a clever, dedicated cop of the worst type. A man who had instincts and believed in them, who clung to his own ideas tenaciously in spite of logic, or evidence. This then was the real reason Convery had been visiting John Breton at intervals over the past nine years – he was suspicious. What vindictive twist of fate, Breton wondered, had brought this ambling super-cop on to the stage he had so carefully set on that October night?

'Lost a shoe?'

'A shoe?' Breton followed Convery's gaze and saw the black slip-on gripped in his own hand. 'Oh yes. I'm getting absent-minded.'

'We all do when we have something on our minds – look at that fossil.'

'I don't have anything on my mind,' Breton said immediately. 'What's troubling you?'

Convery walked to the Lincoln and leaned against it, his right hand resting on the lid of the trunk. 'Nothing much – I keep trying to talk with my hand.'

'I don't get it.'

'It's nothing. By the way – speaking of hands – those knuckles of yours are looking a bit raw. Have you been in a fight or something?'

'Who with?' Breton laughed. 'I can't fight myself.'

'Well, I thought maybe the guy who delivered your car.' Convery slapped the metal and the unsecured lid of the trunk vibrated noisily. 'The way those grease-monkeys speak to customers I often feel like belting them myself – that's one of the reasons I do all my own maintenance.'

Breton felt his mouth go dry. So Convery had noticed the car had not been around on his earlier visit. 'No,' he said. 'I'm on the best of terms with my service station.'

'What were you getting done to her?' Convery eyed the Lincoln with a practical man's disdain.

'Brakes needed adjusting.'

'Is that so? I thought the brakes on these things were self-adjusting.'

'Perhaps they are – I never looked to see.' Breton began to wonder how long this could go on. 'All I know is she wasn't stopping too well.'

'Do you want some advice? Make sure the wheels are bolted on properly before you take her out on the road. I've seen cars come back from a brake job with the wheels' nuts hanging on by a single thread.'

'I'm sure it'll be all right.'

'Don't trust 'em, John – if there's anything they can leave loose without it actually falling off, they'll do it.'

Convery suddenly uncoiled himself and whipped around to the rear of the car before Breton could move. He caught the handle of the trunk lid, raised it – staring triumphantly at Breton – and slammed it down hard, twisting the handle into the locked position.

'See what I mean? That could have sprung up while you were travelling fast – very dangerous.'

'Thanks,' Breton said faintly. 'I'm obliged.'

'Think nothing of it – all part of the service to the tax-payers.' Convery pulled thoughtfully on one of his ears. 'Well, I've got to go. My kids are having a birthday party, and I'm not supposed to be out at all. Be seeing you.'

'Any time,' Breton replied. 'Look me up any time.'

He waited uncertainly, then followed Convery around the side of the house, reaching the front in time to see a green saloon surge down the street with a grumbling of exhausts. A cool breeze scattered dry leaves before him as he turned and walked back to the car. Convery's last remark had been a significant one. It had revealed that his call had been neither social nor accidental, and Convery was unlikely to give away information without a reason. Breton was left with the distinct impression that he had been given a warning – which left him in a strange and potentially lethal situation.

He could not risk killing John Breton with Lieutenant Convery possibly circling the block, waiting for something to happen.

Yet he could not let John Breton live after what had happened – and there was very little time in which to resolve the dilemma.

ELEVEN

SEVERAL DECADES HAD gone by since General Theodor Abram had actually set foot on a field of battle, but he thought of himself as living in an ephemeral no-man's-land separating two of the greatest war machines ever seen in the region's ancient and bloody history.

There was never an hour, a minute, a single instant in which his mind was not dominated by the realization that he was a vital part of his country's front line defences. If the ultimate conflict was ever joined he would not be required to press any buttons; the tools of his trade were made of paper, not steel; but he was a warrior nonetheless because the burden of responsibility for technical preparedness was such that only a patriot and a hero could have borne it.

The nightmare of General Abram's life was compounded by the fact that he had two entirely separate sets of enemies.

One was the nation against whom his own people might some day be called to arms; the other set was represented by his own missiles and the technicians who designed and maintained them. A scarred fortress of a man, intended by nature for fighting with broadsword and mace, he had little instinct for technological warfare and even less for the interminable waiting which was the alternative. As far as possible he avoided making personal visits to the underground bases – too often, seven out of a batch of eight missiles would have malfunctionings in their incredibly complex innards. The technicians in charge seemed oblivious to the thought that these 'minor defects' and the subsequent replacement and testing procedures were reducing the country's initial strike power to a fraction of its nominal value.

Abram could not understand why a ballistic missile had

to have something like a million parts; still less could he fathom the mathematics of reliability which dictated that the assembly of individually trustworthy components in such large numbers invariably produced a wilful, capricious entity whose effectiveness could vary from minute to minute. During his years in office he had developed a profound dislike for the scientists and engineers who had inflicted his present circumstances on him, and he took every opportunity to show it.

He glanced at his watch. Dr Rasch, chief scientist in the Defence Ministry, had phoned earlier for an appointment and was due to arrive at any second. The thought of having to endure the little man's thin, overly precise tones so late in the afternoon made General Abram's already taut nerves sing like high tension cables in a storm. When he heard the outer door of his office open, he leaned forward on his desk, scowling, ready to crush the scientist by the sheer weight of his hatred.

'Good afternoon, General,' Dr Rasch said as he was shown in. 'It was most kind of you to see me at such short notice.'

'Afternoon.' Abram looked closely at Rasch, wondering what had happened. The little man's yellowed eyes had a strange light in them. It could have been fear, relief, or even triumph. 'What's the news?'

'I don't quite know how to tell you, General.' Abram suddenly realized that Rasch was enjoying himself, and his depression grew even deeper. They must have found a design flaw in some component – a pump perhaps, or a microscopic valve – which demanded retrospective modification to every installation.

'I hope you'll find someway to express yourself,' Abram said heavily. 'Otherwise your visit seems rather pointless.'

Rasch's lean face twitched violently. 'The difficulty is not in my powers of expression, but in your powers of comprehension.' Even in anger, Rasch still spoke with carefully measured pedantry.

'Make it very simple for me,' Abram challenged.

'Very well. I presume you've noticed the meteor shower which has been going on for some time now?'

'Very pretty,' Abram sneered. 'Is that what you came to discuss with me?'

'Indirectly. Have you learned what's causing this unprecedented display?'

'If I have, I've forgotten it already. I have no time for scientific trivialities.'

'Then I'll remind you.' Rasch had recovered his poise – a fact which Abram found vaguely disturbing. 'There is now no doubt that the force of gravity is decreasing. The Earth normally travels in an orbit which it has long ago swept clear of cosmic debris, but with the new change in the gravitic constant the orbit is becoming cluttered again – partly as a result of displacement of the planet, even more so as a result of the apparently greater effect on minute bodies. The meteor displays are visual evidence that gravity—'

'Gravity, gravity!' Abram shouted. 'What do I care about gravity?'

'But you should care, General.' Rasch permitted himself a small, tight smile. 'Gravity is one of the constants in the calculations which the computers in your missiles perform to enable them to reach their designated targets – and now the constant is no longer a constant.'

'You mean ...' Abram broke off as the enormity of Rasch's words got through to him.

'Yes, General. The missiles won't land precisely on the selected targets.'

'But you can allow for this change in gravity, surely.'

'Of course, but it's going to take some time. The decrease is progressive, and—'

'How long?'

Rasch shrugged carelessly. 'Six months, perhaps. It all depends.'

'But this places me in an impossible situation. What will the President say?'

'I wouldn't venture a guess, General – but we all have one consolation.'

'Which is?'

'Every nation in the world is facing the same problem. You

are worried about a comparative handful of short-range missiles – think how the Russians and the Americans and the others must be feeling.' Rasch had acquired an air of dreamy, philosophical calm which Abram found infuriating.

'And what about you, Dr Rasch?' he said. 'Aren't you worried too?'

'Worried, General, worried?' Rasch stared out through the window to where the desert was shimmering in the day's still-growing heat. 'If you have time to listen, I'll explain how these scientific trivialities – as you term them – are going to affect the future of humanity.'

He began to speak in a thin, strangely wistful monotone. And, as he listened, General Abram discovered the *real* meaning of fear ...

On almost any clear night on Ridgeway Street, especially if there was a moon, an open window could be seen at the top of the highest house.

People out late sometimes saw a pale blur moving in the oblong of darkness and knew they had caught Willy Lucas watching them. And Willy, his pimply fuzz-covered face twisted with panic, would lunge back from the window, afraid of being seen.

The women who lived opposite often thought Willy was trying to spy into their bedrooms, and had had him punished by complaining to his brother. But Willy was not interested in the tight-lipped, bleak-eyed housewives of Ridgeway Street, nor even in the strange and alluring females who sometimes walked near him in dreams.

The truth was that Willy enjoyed looking out across the silent town when all others had gone to sleep. It was, for those treasured hours, as though they had died and left him alone, and there was nobody to shout or look at him with exasperation ...

When the first of the meteors began to fall Willy was at his post high in the tall, narrow building. Quivering with excitement, he snatched up his old mother-of-pearl opera glasses, stolen from Cooney's junk store on the corner, and focused them into the dark bowl of the sky. Each time he saw a meteor, its transient brilliance limned with prismatic colour by the damaged optical system of his glasses, formless and disturbing thoughts stirred in his mind. With the alert instincts of one not altogether at home in the normal pattern of existence, he realized that the fugitive motes of light carried a special message just for him – but what could it be?

Willy watched until near dawn, crouched in the freezing darkness of the little attic, then he closed the window and went to bed.

When he woke up and came down for lunch the grocery store at the front of the house was crowded. His two older sisters, Ada and Emily, were too busy to come back and prepare a meal for him so Willy made sandwiches with mashed banana thickly spread with marmalade.

As he munched in silent abstraction he hardly saw the pages of the book he was leafing through, or heard the sliding rumble of potatoes being weighed in the store. For, just as in the Bible, it had come to him in his sleep – the awful, heart-stilling significance of the falling stars.

He felt uplifted at having been chosen as the instrument whereby the message would be spread throughout the world, but there was also a vast responsibility. Willy had never in his life carried even the smallest shred of responsibility, and he was uncertain about his own capabilities – especially in a matter of such importance. He drifted around the dark, shabby house all day, trying to think of a way to discharge his God-given obligations, but was unable to decide on any worthwhile plan.

At dusk, his brother Joe came home from his job in the town's gas plant, and was angry because Willy had not whitewashed the yard. Willy paid little attention to him, accepting the furious words meekly, while his mind sought dimly for a way in which to honour God's trust.

That night the meteor display was even more brilliant than before, and Willy began to feel an unaccustomed sense of urgency, almost a feeling of guilt that he had done nothing about spreading the Word. He began to worry, and when

Willy was absentminded it effectively reduced him to a state of imbecility. Once while mooning around the store he knocked over a basket of tomatoes, and another time dropped a crate of empty Coca-Cola bottles on the tiled floor.

Another night of teeming brilliance had passed before the idea came to him. It was a miserable little idea, he realized – achieving some degree of objectivity – but no doubt God understood the limitations of His chosen instrument better than did Willy himself.

Once he understood what he had to do, Willy became impatient to go on with his work. Instead of drifting off to sleep after his nightly vigil, he hurried downstairs and out to the back yard in search of woodworking tools. Joe was standing at the stove, already dressed in stained brown overalls, gulping tea. He looked up at Willy with his usual expression of dismayed hatred.

'Willy,' he said tersely. 'If you don't get the whitewashing done today, I'll do the job myself, and you'll be the brush.'

'Yes, Joe.'

'I'm warning you for the last time, Willy. We're all sick of you not even lifting a finger to pay for your keep.'

'Yes, Joe.'

'You lie in bed all night and half the day too.'

'Yes, Joe.'

Willy stared down into his brother's square, competent face and was tempted to reveal just how fortunate it had been for Joe, Ada, Emily and everyone else in the world that he had *not* been lying in bed all night. Thanks to his vigilance they had all gained a little time. But he decided against saying anything too soon, and went on out to the yard.

The work proved more difficult than Willy had anticipated, one of the first snags being the scarcity of suitable materials. He wasted some time pawing through the heap of rain-blackened lumber at the end of the yard, hurting his fingers on its slippery solidity, covering his clothes with mossy green smears and flecks of orange-red fungus. Finally he realized there was nothing for him in the pile, and went into the outhouse which Ada and Emily used as a storeroom.

Near the door was a large plywood packing case filled with paper bags and squares of brown paper for wrapping vegetables. He began lifting the contents out carefully but the blocks of paper were unexpectedly weighty and hard to control with his numb fingers. They kept falling to the ground and bursting apart. Willy endured the inanimate perversity for as long as he could, then he upended the packing case, releasing a pulpy avalanche which slithered out to the muddy concrete of the yard.

It doesn't matter much now, he thought.

Even when he had the packing case torn apart, the job refused to go well. The thin plywood kept splintering or reverting to separate laminations when he tried to cut it, and nail heads continually passed right through it. He worked on determinedly, not pausing to eat or even to dash the sweat from his fuzz-covered face, until by late afternoon he had completed a shaky structure which roughly matched his requirements.

Pangs of hunger were twisting his stomach, but he had been lucky that neither Ada nor Emily had poked her bespectacled face through the back door all day, and he decided to press on with his task. He found a can of red paint and a brush, and went to work with them, occasionally moaning softly as he gave the job all the concentration of which his mind was capable.

It was past five by the time he had finished and – since he had to let the paint dry, anyway – he decided to clean himself up and get something to eat. He loped up the dark stairs, washed his face and feverishly changed into his Sunday suit, which seemed appropriate for the occasion. Satisfying himself that there was still some daylight left, Willy ran back down to the ground floor, panting with eagerness.

In the narrow passage behind the store he collided with the blocky figure of Joe, who had just come in from work.

'Well?' Joe's voice was taut with suppressed anger. 'Have you done it?'

Willy stared down at him, aghast. He had completely forgotten the whitewashing. 'Ah ... There wasn't time. I been busy.'

'I thought so.' Joe caught hold of Willy's lapels and pushed him towards the rear of the house, using all his adult strength. 'Get the job done right now, or I'll kill you, Willy. I'll *kill* you!'

Joe opened the back door, threw Willy out into the yard and slammed the door behind him. Willy looked around helplessly for a moment, eyes brimming with tears, then he ran to the shed and got the covered bucket of whitewash and a broad brush. He attacked the job ferociously, splashing the bubbling liquid on to the old uneven bricks in long curving strokes, heedless of his clothes. An hour later the walls were all coated and Willy, aching and blistered, set the bucket aside. At that precise moment, the door opened and Joe came out.

'I'm sorry I was so rough on you, Willy.' Joe sounded tired. 'You'd better come in and have something to eat.'

'I don't want nothing,' Willy replied.

'Look, I said I was sorry ...' Joe's voice trailed away as he noticed the scurf of trampled paper around the outhouse door. Then his gaze reached the object Willy had spent all day building, and his jaw dropped. 'What the hell?'

'Stay away!'

Willy felt a pang of alarm as he assessed Joe's reaction to what he had seen, and knew that the way ahead was not going to be easy. He brushed Joe aside and ran towards his creation. Joe grappled with him but Willy, filled with divine anger, hurled him aside with one arm. From the corner of his eye he saw Joe tumble into the pile of timber, and he felt a surge of triumphant conviction. He lifted the flimsy structure, placed it over his shoulders and strode purposefully into the house. Women shoppers screamed as he burst out into the store on his way to the street. Willy was only dimly aware of the screams, or of the startled grey faces of his sisters behind the counter. For the first time in his life, he had a real place in the world, with something important to do, and nothing was going to stop him.

He was also only dimly aware of the futile sound of brakes

as he thrust his way out on to the street, of the automobile's slewing rush, of the bone-crushing impact. And a few seconds later he was aware of nothing at all.

People rushing to view the accident trampled unseeingly over the boards which Willy had so laboriously constructed. None of them read the crudely printed words:

'THE END IS NIGH – PREPARE TO MEET THY DOOM.'

'... but,' General Abram was saying, 'if all this is true it means ...'

Dr Rasch nodded dreamily. 'That is correct, General. It means the end of the world.'

TWELVE

AS SOON AS he had reached his decision, Breton locked up the house and hurried to the car.

He had no real idea how long Kate would stay with the Palfreys, but it was vital for him to get back first if she was to believe that John had walked out. The fishing lodge was nearly forty miles to the north. It was not far for the big Turbo-Lincoln, but there were arrangements to be made once he got there and he would not be able to drive too fast in case he attracted the attention of the highway patrol. He could be unlucky enough to encounter the mobile equivalent of Lieutenant Convery.

The car quivered gently as he pushed the turbine spin-up button, then it settled into a kind of alert silence. Only the position of indicator needles showed the engine was turning. Breton slid the car out on to the street, pointed it north and brought his foot down on the throttle. The resultant surge of acceleration snapped his head back and he eased his foot up again, suddenly respectful of the power he was controlling.

He drove carefully, working north by west, until he had reached the main Silverstream highway, where a small movement of his right foot brought the speed up to sixty without any perceptible increase in engine note. A good machine, he thought appreciatively. The complementary thought that the car was already his flickered in the back of his mind, but he kept it there.

As he reached the outskirts of the city Breton distracted himself by looking for visible difference between the Time B world and his memory of the same area in Time A. But things appeared no different – there was the same penumbra of lumber yards, used-car lots, lonely little banks stranded far away from their parent organizations, knots of bravely-lit stores, diners, and occasional incongruous groups of houses. The same straggling slob land he had always known and detested, exactly repeated. Altering a few human lives had left the city untouched, he realized.

When the car had shaken off the city and was arrowing through the Montana prairie, Breton increased speed, and insects began to splatter the windshield. A coppery sun was setting to his left, withdrawing its light from a peacock-green sky. Far off to the east something flickered above the horizon and he instinctively covered his right eye, expecting to find the teichopsia that usually preceded one of his attacks. But this time there were no prismatic fortifications, and when he took his hand away he knew the glimmer in the sky had been a meteor. So the showers are still going on, he thought. And what else is happening?

Some people are becoming telepathic, satellites are drifting out of place, the solar radiation is affecting radio communications, religious cranks are predicting the end of the world ...

Something moved at the rear of the car. Breton, who had been reaching for the radio to see if he could pick up a newscast, froze and listened intently, but the faint sound was not repeated. John Breton must have been stirring in his sleep, he decided. He switched the radio on.

'... *of NASA has recommended that all airlines operating supersonic transports should restrict their operational ceiling to fifty thousand feet until further notified. This limitation has been imposed by the reported sharp increase in cosmic radiation which scientists regard as a health-hazard for passengers on long-distance, high altitude flights. In Washington DC this morning . . .'*

Breton switched off quickly, feeling that somehow his future with Kate was being threatened. The need for her was stirring in his body again, and tonight they would be alone in the house. Memories of that first open-mouthed kiss, visions of Kate's breasts suddenly alive and free in their escape from the nylon harness, of ivory-textured thighs – a sensual montage filled Breton's mind, making it impossible for him to think about anything other than the all important miracle of Kate's existence.

He forced himself to concentrate on immediate necessities, keeping the tracer-stream of white road markers accurately below the car's left wing, occasionally washing the shattered insects from the windshield. But she was there before him, all the while, and he knew he would never again let go of her.

The sun had dropped below the horizon by the time he reached the shores of Lake Pasco and angled off the highway along the narrower road which dipped through a stand of pines. Dusk closed in, ambushing the car as soon as he got down among the trees. Breton negotiated two minor crossroads, anxiously aware that it was at least twelve years since he had been in the area. There was an ivy-covered fishing lodge on the south shore which he had always admired, even though it had been far beyond his income in those days. He *thought* that would be the one John Breton would have bought after he prospered – but this was one facet in which Time B really could be divergent. Suppose John's tastes had changed?

Cursing himself for not having pinned down the location of the lodge exactly, while he had the chance, Breton steered the car down a deserted, half-remembered track and reached a cleared space at the water's edge. He swung around on the pebbly surface and parked between the single-storied lodge and a green-painted boathouse. The cold, moist air from the lake insinuated itself under his clothing as soon as he got out of the car. Shivering slightly, he took the keys from his pocket and went to the door of the dark-windowed lodge.

The third key he tried turned the lock. He pushed the door open and went back to the car and lifted the lid of the trunk. John Breton was lying curled on his side. He looked ill, and the choking, biscuity smell of urine rose up around him, making Jack flinch guiltily. His other self had been left with nothing, not even dignity, and Jack too felt sullied. He dragged the unconscious man from the metallic cave of the trunk and, holding him under his arms, trailed him to the lodge. As they were going up the three steps at the door, John mumbled something and began to struggle feebly.

'You'll be all right,' Jack whispered inanely. 'Just relax.'

The lodge's central room was furnished with deep, tweed-covered chairs. A neo-rustic dining table and wooden chairs were clustered at the window which overlooked the lake. Four doors opened off the room. Jack chose the one which looked as though it would lead to the basement, and his guess proved correct. He left John lying on the floor and flipped the light switch at the head of the wooden stairs, but the darkness below remained. A quick search of the room revealed a main switch hidden in a cupboard. He threw the lever and saw yellow brilliance spill from the basement door.

As he was being eased downstairs, John Breton began to struggle again. Jack tried to restrain him and keep balance for the both of them at the same time, but he found himself in danger of a serious fall. He released his grip on John, letting him jar his way helplessly down the remaining steps. John hit the concrete floor of the basement with a solid thud and lay without moving. One of his black slip-on shoes was still missing.

Jack Breton stepped over him and went to a work-bench at one side on which some engine parts were sitting. He opened the bench's long drawer and found what he was looking for – a spool of fishing line. The label confirmed that the line was of the recently developed locked-molecule variety which looked like finest sewing thread and had a breaking strain measured in thousands of pounds. He cut off two lengths, employing the special pressure-guillotine provided on the spool, and used one piece to tie John's wrists together behind his back. The other, longer piece he worked through one of the ceiling joists, tied it securely and bound the other end around John's arm, above the elbow. He dropped the spool in his pocket to eliminate any chance of John getting hold of it later and escaping.

'What are you doing to me?' John's voice was blurred, but it had a kind of tired reasonableness. It came just as Jack was clamping the final knot.

'I'm tying you up so you won't be any trouble.'

'I guessed that. But why did you bring me here? Why am I not dead?' In his drugged, dazed condition, John sounded only mildly interested.

'Convery came around today – twice. I got worried about him.'

'I don't blame you.' John tried to laugh. 'Especially if he came twice – he never did that before, not even when he was trying to pin Spiedel's death on me. He has read your soul. Convery reads souls, you know ...' John broke off to retch, turning his face to the dusty floor, and Jack felt a sudden dismay. An idea was half-formed in his mind. He went upstairs, out to the car and brought in the two cases full of John's clothes. John was still lying on his side, but he was conscious, his eyes watchful.

'Why the cases?'

'You've just walked out of your marriage.'

'You think she'll believe it?'

'She'll believe it when you don't come back.'

'I see.' John lapsed into silence for a moment. 'You're going to keep me here till you're sure you're in the clear with Convery, and then ...'

'That's right.' Jack set the cases down. 'And then ...'

'That's great,' John said bitterly. 'That's bloody great. You know you're a maniac, don't you?'

'I've already explained my position. I gave you nine years of life.'

'You gave me nothing. It happened as a ... as a by-product of your own schemes.'

'It happened just the same.'

'If you think that reconciles me to the prospect of being murdered – it *proves* you're a maniac.' John closed his eyes momentarily. 'You're a sick man. Jack. And you're wasting your time.'

'Why?'

'The only reason you got a toehold with Kate and me was that we were ripe for somebody like you to come along. But Kate'll see through you any day – and when that happens she'll run. She'll run hard, Jack.'

Jack stared down at his other self. 'You're trying to talk your way out of this. It won't work. This isn't one of your old movies.'

'I know. I know it's real. Remember the way Grand-dad Breton looked that morning I ... we ... found him in bed?'

Jack nodded. Involuntary propulsion of the eyeballs, they had called it. He had been eight years old at the time, and the technical jargon had not been much comfort.

'I remember.'

'That morning, I decided never to die.'

'I know. Do you think I don't know?' Jack took a deep breath. 'Listen, why don't you cut out?'

'What do you mean?'

'If I let you go – would you take off? Would you vanish altogether and leave Kate and me alone?' Having uttered the words, Jack felt an overwhelming surge of benevolence towards his other self. This was the way to handle the situation – surely John would gladly accept life elsewhere in preference to death here in this basement. He watched John's reactions carefully.

'Of course I would.' John's eyes became alive. 'I'd go anywhere – I'm not stupid.'

'Well, then.'

The two men looked into each other's faces and Jack Breton felt something very strange take place inside his head. His mind and John Breton's mind *touched*. The contact was fleeting and feather-light, yet frightening. It was the first time anything remotely like it had ever happened to him, but he understood it with perfect certitude. He understood, too, that John had been lying to him when he said he was prepared to bow out.

'I suppose we were naturals for this telepathy thing that seems to be going around,' John said quietly. 'Our brains must be practically identical, after all.'

'I'm sorry.'

'I'm not. I'm almost grateful to you, in fact. I didn't realize how much Kate meant to me, but now I know – and it's too much to let me walk out and leave her to someone like you.'

'Even if the alternative is dying?'

'Even if the alternative is dying.' John Breton managed to smile as he spoke.

'So be it,' Jack said flatly. 'So be it.'

'You weren't going to let me go, anyway.'

'I . . .'

'Telepathy is a two-way thing, Jack. A moment ago I found out as much about you as you did about me. You're convinced you couldn't really take the risk of having me running around loose – and there's something else.'

'Such as?' Jack Breton had an uneasy feeling that he was losing the initiative in a conversation in which he ought to have been completely on top.

'At heart, you *want* to kill me. I represent your own guilt. You're in the unique position of being able to pay the supreme penalty – by executing me – yet to live on.'

'That, if I may coin a phrase, is double-talk.'

'It isn't. I don't know what you went through after Kate died in your time-stream, but it made you into a psychological cripple, Jack. When you're faced with a problem you blind yourself to all solutions except the one which satisfies your own need to kill.'

'Nonsense.' Jack Breton began making sure the curtains on the basement's small windows were well secured.

'You've demonstrated this already – by your own admission.' John was beginning to sound drowsy.

'Go on.'

'When you made that big trip back through time – there was no need for you to take a rifle and shoot Spiedel. You could have accomplished as much, or more, by going back to the scene of that stupid row I had with Kate when the car broke down. All you had to do was warn me.'

'I thought I had explained the limitations of chronomotive physics to you,' Jack replied. 'There is no conscious selection of destination – the mind is drawn towards the key event, the turning point.'

'Precisely what I'm saying! I'm a victim of *hemicrania sine dolore*, too. I've seen the marching coloured angles dozens of times in the last nine years, and I've made dozens of trips – always to the scene of the argument, because I knew that was where it started. That was where my guilt lay, but you couldn't face that, Jack.

'You accepted it for a while, then – you told us about it the night you arrived at the house – you began to focus on the scene of the killing. You began to see the trees of the park projecting up through the traffic lanes. The reason was that the murder scene had a powerful attraction for you. It had Spiedel – a ready-made vehicle for the transference of your guilt; it was a moment of danger for Kate – in which there was no time to weigh up right and wrong. There was only time to kill . . .'

'You're wrong,' Jack whispered.

'Face up to it, Jack – it's your only chance. You and I were one man at that time, so I know what lay right at the back of your mind. You *wanted* Kate to die. When Convery came to the door that first time you heard the same inner voice as I did, the one telling you you had been set free. But there's nothing so terrible about it . . .' John's eyes closed again, and his voice began to fade. '. . . You can't love a woman without wanting to kill her sometime . . . she won't always be what you want her to be . . . sometimes she wants to be herself . . . trick is to learn to adjust . . . you gotta adjust . . .' John Breton fell asleep, his bruised face pressed against the floor.

'You fool,' Jack said. 'You poor fool.'

He went up the stairs and paused with his hand on the light switch, checking the arrangements he had made to keep John imprisoned. When the other man recovered consciousness he would be able to move around the central part of the basement, but he would be unable to reach any tools with which he might free himself. John Breton would be extremely uncomfortable, Jack reflected grimly, but it would not be for very long. He clicked out the light and went back outside, carefully locking the door of the lodge behind him.

It had grown much darker while he was inside, but the sky was literally alive with light. Above the northern horizon, ghostly curtains of red and green brilliance spread their shimmering folds across the heavens, twitching and flailing in response to the awesome solar winds. The aurora was so bright that it screened out the polar stars. Familiar constellations shone in the rest of the sky, but they too had dimmed in comparison to the vast, silent pyrotechnics of the meteor display. The night world was being bombarded with fire by a frantic giant, divergent showers tracing their paths across the atmospheric shield in an unsteady rhythm, punctuated by brighter projectiles which spanned the horizons in mind-quailing arcs.

The whole fantastic scene was reflected in the waters of the lake, turning its surface into a seething mirror. Breton faced it unseeingly for a moment, then got into the car. His hand brushed against a smooth, dark object lying on the front seat. It was John Breton's shoe – the one which had caught Lieutenant Convery's attention earlier in the day. Opening the window, he threw the shoe out towards the water, but it fell short and he heard it bounce on the pebbles. He shrugged, started the car and slewed it around in a gravel-spitting circle.

Driving south on the Silverstream highway, he found himself continually glancing in the mirror with a feeling of being followed – even though there was nothing behind but the pulsing lights of the aurora.

THIRTEEN

BRETON WAS RELIEVED to find the house in darkness when he got back.

He put the car in the garage and went into the house by the back door. A glance at his watch showed him that he had been away less than three hours – it had seemed much longer. Walking through the hall, he noticed the bottle of sleeping tablets lying where he had thrown it. He picked it up and took it back to the bathroom.

The sight of himself in the bathroom mirror gave Breton a shock. His face was haggard and shaded with stubble, his clothing rumpled and streaked with dust. He looked around the room and noted with approval that, as well as a shower stall, it was fitted with a deep tub. While hot water was thundering from the tap, he searched closets and produced clean underwear, a soft, dark-green shirt and a pair of slacks belonging to John Breton. He carried them into the bathroom, locked the door and proceeded to have the hottest bath he could remember. Half an hour later he was clean, relaxed and freshly-shaven – and it felt good.

He went downstairs into the friendly, soft-toned spaciousness of the big living-room and stood, hesitating, before the cocktail cabinet. He had been avoiding alcohol almost completely for years because, as far as he was concerned, drinking and hard work were mutually exclusive. But that phase of his life had passed – he had now achieved just about everything he had set out to achieve, and could afford to relax a little. He inspected the whisky, found it was Johnny Walker Black Label and nodded in satisfaction. John and he had diverged in many ways over the nine years, but his other self was still a good judge of liquor. He poured a generous measure, carried it over to the deepest armchair and began sipping. The evocative aroma, and the warmth of distilled sunlight seeping through his system, relaxed him still further. He took another glass ...

Breton awoke with a start of panic, wondering where he was. It took several seconds for his surroundings to register, and when they did, he felt worried. The wall clock told him it was past two in the morning, and obviously Kate had not come home yet. He got to his feet, shivering after the long sleep, then heard the faint sound of the garage door being closed. Kate had arrived, after all, and the sound of her car's high-compression engine coming up the drive must have been what had awakened him.

Self-consciously, nervously, he went through to the back of the house and opened the kitchen door. She came towards the light, the belt of her tweed suit untied and the jacket lying open to reveal the horizontal tensions of her tangerine-coloured sweater. Breton had never seen Kate look so much like Kate.

'John,' she said uncertainly, shielding her eyes. 'Oh ... Jack.'

'Come in, Kate,' he said gently. 'John has gone.'

'Gone?'

'Well, I did warn you. I told you the sort of mood he was in today.'

'I know you did – but I didn't expect ... Are you sure he's gone? The car's still out in the garage.'

'He took a taxi. To the airport, I think. He wasn't communicative.'

Kate peeled off her gloves and dropped them on the kitchen table. Breton automatically locked the kitchen door, like an ordinary husband sealing up his little fortress for the night, then found Kate staring at him, sombrely, in a way which invested his familiar action with significance. He made a show of carelessly flinging the key on to the table, and ensured that it ended up nestling into the fingers of her gloves. What a start, he thought. A clash of symbols.

'I don't understand,' she said. 'You mean he's just walked out? For good?'

'This is what I was warning you about, Kate. John was reaching the point where he had to make some pretty massive adjustments to his emotional circumstances. He probably interpreted you staying away from the house today as a lack of concern.' Breton made himself sound contrite. 'You can imagine how I feel.'

Kate walked through to the living-room and stood at the stone chimney, staring down into the unlit fire. Breton followed her and positioned himself at the other side of the room, carefully gauging her reactions. A too sudden advance at this stage could trigger off the antagonism he had noticed in her earlier in the day. Kate had a conscience.

'You're wearing John's clothes,' she said, almost abstractedly.

'He took all he wanted and left me the rest.' Breton was amazed to find himself on the defensive. 'He filled two cases.'

'But what about the business? Are you? . . .'

'That's John's idea. I take it over.'

'You would.' Kate's eyes were unreadable.

Breton decided it was time to shift his attack. 'I don't want you to get the idea that John's completely unhappy about all this. He's been feeling trapped – by his career and marriage – for years. Now he isn't trapped. He's made an effortless, guilt-free escape from a situation that was becoming intolerable to him, and it didn't even cost him divorce fees.'

'Just a million dollar business.'

'The point is, he didn't have to quit the business. I didn't come here looking for money, Kate. I threw away every cent I owned, just to reach you.'

Kate turned to face him and her voice had softened. 'I know. I'm sorry I said that. So much has happened.'

Breton moved towards her and put his hands on her shoulders. 'Kate, darling, I . . .'

'Don't do that,' she said quietly.

'I *am* your husband.'

'There are times when I don't want my husband to touch me.'

'Of course.'

Breton let his arms fall by his sides. He had a feeling he had been taking part in an undeclared battle, and that Kate had won it through sheer superior generalship.

During the long hours of that night, as he lay alone in the guest room, he was brought face-to-face with a disturbing truth. Nine years of separate existence in the Time B world had left their mark on Kate, making her a different person than the girl he had lost and conquered Time itself to recover.

And there was nothing in the whole wide universe he could do about it.

FOURTEEN

BRETON HAD FORGOTTEN that the days of the week existed.

Consequently he was surprised, on opening his eyes in buttery morning sunlight, to be immediately aware that the day was Saturday. He lay, between consciousness and sleep, considering the implications of his apparently *a priori* knowledge.

Of the four major divisions of time – day, week, month and year – week was the odd man out. All the others were based on recurring astronomical phenomena, but the week was a purely human measure, the distance between market days. An alert animal waking from sleep might be expected to know the position of the sun, the phase of the Moon, or the season – but to be aware of Saturday? Unless his subsconscious had its own seven-day clock, or had picked up a variation in the pattern of traffic sounds drifting through the partially-open window . . .

Breton came fully awake as his mind reorientated itself. He wondered fleetingly what sort of a night John Breton had passed, then fended the thought away. Last night he had been forced by Kate to play the role of a gentle, reasonable friend of the family; but it had been a mistake not to consummate his new marriage right away. He was giving Kate too much time to think her own thoughts and arrive at conclusions unaffected by the dictates of passion. Words like union and congress had a special significance in this context because, once the sexual amalgamation had been achieved, Kate's conscience – at the moment a free agent – would be obliged to justify the new state of affairs. Certain avenues of thought would be barred to her, and Breton wanted them closed as soon as possible.

He got up and opened the bedroom door. The irregular whine of a vacuum cleaner drifted up the stairs, showing that Kate was up and about. He washed, shaved and dressed as quickly as possible, and went downstairs. The sound of the cleaner had stopped but there was movement in the kitchen. Hesitating a moment to get his tactics clear in his mind, he pushed the door open and walked in.

'It's Mr Breton,' a small, blue-haired woman said brightly. 'Good morning, Mr Breton.'

Breton gaped at her in amazement. The strange woman was sitting at the table, having coffee with Kate. She was about sixty, wore bright red lipstick and had a crack in the right-hand lens of her spectacles.

'Mrs Fitz came by to see how we were getting along without her,' Kate explained. 'And when she saw the mess the place was in, she insisted on cleaning it up right away. I've been getting a lecture for neglecting you.'

'Very good of you, Mrs Fitz,' Breton mumbled. The housekeeper! He had forgotten all about the damned housekeeper. Mrs Fitz regarded him with frank, shiny-eyed curiosity as he edged his way around the table to a vacant chair. He gave her a wan smile.

'Mr Breton's lost weight.' Mrs Fitz spoke to Kate as though he were not there. 'Mr Breton's got thinner. That settles it – no more days off for me!'

'It has been a bit of a strain without you,' Kate said. 'John doesn't care much for my cooking.'

'Nonsense.' Breton looked at her helplessly, masking his rage. 'You know I love your cooking. I don't think we ought to monopolize Mrs Fitz's weekend.'

'Listen to him!' Mrs Fitz laughed, showing incredibly white dentures. 'As if I had anything better to do.'

'How is your niece?' Kate asked warmly. 'Has she had her baby yet?'

'Not yet.'

Mrs Fitz got up and began to serve Breton with coffee, pancakes and syrup as she spoke. He ate silently, marvelling at the way one or two words from Kate, interposed at the right places, could act as verbal catalysts for the older woman, drawing longer and longer skeins of words from her. Unable to decide if Kate was doing it on purpose, he endured the conversation for as long as possible then went and sat in the living-room, pretending to read magazines.

After the breakfast things were cleaned up, the vacuum cleaner started up again and Mrs Fitz began to go over the whole house, appearing – to Breton's inflamed senses – to do some of the rooms several times. Kate spent a lot of time talking to her, and came into the living-room alone only once, carrying a vase of flowers.

'For God's sake, get rid of that woman,' he said. 'I've got to talk to you.'

'I'm trying to – but Mrs Fitz was always like this.'

Kate sounded genuinely concerned, and he tried to relax. The morning dragged past and, to his dismay, Mrs Fitz stayed on and made lunch. After they had eaten, there was the prolonged routine of tidying up and then, incredulously, Breton heard the vacuum cleaner whine into life again. He threw his magazine aside and bulled his way upstairs, following the sound. Kate was standing at the door of a bedroom, smoking, and Mrs Fitz was at work inside.

'What's she doing now?' he demanded. 'The floors can't have got dirty since this morning.'

Kate dropped her cigarette into a cut-glass ashtray she had carried with her. 'The drapes. Mrs Fitz likes to do the drapes on Saturdays.'

Breton started to turn away; but then he realized that Kate – mature and experienced skirmisher that she had become – was calmly manipulating him, practising a kind of super-judo which turned his strength into weakness. And he had been tamely knuckling under, in spite of the fact that the only lever she had was the knowledge he had given her. But *as far as she knew*, the knowledge was useless. She could not go to Mrs Fitz, or anyone else, and tell them the man she was living with was not really her husband, but only a duplicate who had emerged from another time-stream. Not unless she wanted to have her sanity put in doubt.

'Mrs Fitz.' Breton walked past Kate into the bedroom. 'Go home now.'

'Bless you, I'm in no hurry to go back there.'

She gave him a bright smile which conveyed the message that she was a widow gamely carrying on with life's battle. Breton pulled the cord of the cleaner from the socket and handed it to her.

'But I insist.' He smiled as he led her to the door. 'I want you to rest up over the weekend and report for duty good and early on Monday morning. And here's a ten-dollar bonus for being so conscientious, how's that?'

Breton gave her one of the bills he had taken from John, then he escorted Mrs Fitz all the way down the stairs, helped her with her coat and showed her to the door. Her over-red lips worked in silent surprise and she kept glancing back at Kate, but she went – with one final, startled look through the kitchen window as she passed. Breton waved at her.

'That was unforgivable,' Kate said. She had come downstairs behind him.

'I'll be extra nice to her next time,' he replied, going to her. He put his hands on Kate's waist and drew her to him. She came unresistingly and he kissed her. The touch of her lips was light, but enough to restore him, to sweep away the spider-webs of doubt that had begun to cling around his thoughts since the previous day. He closed his eyes, savouring the heady wine of . . . justification.

'I'm worried about John,' Kate said.

'I don't see why.' Breton kept his eyes shut. 'He was happy to walk out on you. Why should you worry about him?'

'Because it was so unlike him, just to vanish like that. He wasn't reacting normally.'

Breton opened his eyes reluctantly. 'He was tired of his

marriage, and he quit. Lots of people would call that a perfectly normal reaction.'

Kate's eyes levelled with his own. 'It was completely unbalanced.'

'How do you figure that?'

'John wouldn't have run off and left everything up in the air – not normally.'

'Well, he did.'

'That's why I'm saying it was a completely unbalanced reaction.'

The repetition of the phrase needled Breton with its inference that there was something wrong with his own mind. 'Don't keep saying that, Kate. It doesn't prove anything.'

She broke away from his arms. 'How about money?'

'Money? You mean for John? I imagine he took plenty.'

'How? Not from our personal account – he didn't ask me to co-sign any cheques. And he didn't have enough time to organize a big withdrawal from the business account.'

'You weren't always such a financial wizard,' Breton said, aware that he sounded like a petulant brat, but unable to hold the words back.

'I lace my own shoes now, too.' Kate spoke with a kind of practised savagery which filled Breton with dismay. Nine years, he suddenly realized, is a long time.

'John will be able to get all the money he wants, just by going to any bank. We'll probably get a letter from him within a few days.'

'A begging letter?'

Breton was not sure when the nightmare had begun, but it had surrounded him just the same. *Kate*, he pleaded silently, *why can you not be what I want you to be?*

She moved restlessly from room to room, picking up small objects and throwing them down again noisily. For a time, Breton followed her in the hope that the mood of their single Venetian-tinted afternoon would miraculously be restored to them. But Kate refused to discuss anything other than John's motives for leaving so abruptly, his possible whereabouts, his future plans. Breton felt helpless. He felt that he ought to be able to confront Kate and draw her to him by the sheer force and intensity of his love, just as he had seemed to do on the night of his arrival – but perhaps his success then had depended on catching a bored, lonely and imaginative woman off guard.

Breton left the house and walked into the gardens. He was astonished to find that the sun was on the horizon – each minute of the day had been insufferably long, but the hours had passed quickly. The air was turning cool, the slow-spreading dyes of night were seeping through the eastern sky, and there already the meteors were beginning to scurry and die like lemmings. As before, the sight of them triggered off vague feelings of alarm. The thought of spending another night alone under a diseased sky was more than Breton could bear.

He walked quickly into the house and slammed the door behind him. Kate was standing in the living-room's bow window, in near-darkness, gazing out at October-coloured trees. She did not turn around as he entered the room. He went to her, gripped her shoulders hard and buried his face in her hair.

'Kate,' he said desperately, 'we're talking too much. We need each other and all we do is talk.'

Kate's body went rigid. 'Please leave me alone.'

'But Kate . . .' He turned her towards him.

'I want you to leave me alone.'

'But this is *us*! Remember that first afternoon . . .'

'This is different.' She broke away from him.

'Why?' he demanded. 'Because there's no chance of John walking in on us? Does that take the flavour out of it?'

Kate hit him across the mouth and, in almost the same instant, he struck back, feeling her teeth cut into his knuckles. The double blow rang out in the silence of the room, but was lost in the thunder inside his head.

'That does it,' Kate snapped. 'Get out of this house.'

'You don't understand,' he mumbled, his mind sinking through regions of cryogenic chill. 'This is my house, and you are my wife.'

'I see.'

Kate spun and left the room. Breton stood absolutely still, staring at his hand in disbelief, until he heard a familiar sound filtering down through the ceiling – the slamming of drawers. He sprinted up to the bedroom above and found Kate throwing clothes into a suitcase.

'What are you doing?'

'I'm getting out of *your* house.'

'There's no need for that.'

'You think not?' Kate's face was grim.

'Of course not – we've both been under a strain. I don't . . .'

'I'm leaving.' Kate slammed the case shut. 'And don't try to stop me.'

'I won't.' Breton's mind was beginning to recover from its paralysis, to analyse his errors. His principal mistake had been to regard Kate as a plum which would drop into his hands as soon as he shook the marital tree. 'I don't know how to apologize for . . .'

'Hitting me? Don't bother – after all, I hit you first.'

'Don't leave me, Kate. It'll never happen again.'

'*I'll* say!' Kate had acquired a defiant jauntiness. She was almost smiling as she turned to face him. 'Promise me something?'

'Anything.'

'If John gets in touch, tell him I must talk to him – I'll be up at Pasco Lake.'

Breton's mouth went dry. 'Where? D'you mean the fishing lodge?'

'Yes.'

'You can't go there.'

'May I ask why?'

'I . . . It's too lonely up there at this time of the year.'

'There are times when I can do without people – and this seems to be one of them.'

'But . . .' Breton found himself floundering helplessly. 'You could stay in town, at an hotel.'

'I like the lake. Please get out of my way.' Kate picked up her case.

'*Kate!*'

Breton raised both hands in front of her, palms turned outwards to form a barrier, while he searched for something meaningful to say. Kate advanced until his hands were almost against her, then the colour drained from her cheeks. He watched in frozen fascination as she made the intuitive leap.

'The lodge,' she breathed. 'John's at the lodge.'

'That's ridiculous.'

'What have you done to him? Why do you want me not to go there?'

'Kate, believe me – you're being silly.'

She nodded calmly, dropped the case at his feet and darted past him. Breton grabbed for her, got one of her elbows and pulled her down on to the bed. She went down kicking and clawing. As he straddled her body, his brain finally produced the one lie which could yet save the situation.

'All right, Kate – you win.' He fought to control the twisting of her body below him. 'You *win*, I tell you.'

'What have you done to John?'

'Nothing. I've given him my chronomotor, that's all. He's up at the lodge learning to use it, so that he can take my place in Time A. It was his own idea, his own way of bowing out.'

'I'm going there.' Kate fought harder, almost toppling him on to the floor.

'Sorry, Kate – not until I've been there first to make sure John has made the crossing.'

Even in the heat of the moment, the weakness of the story appalled him – but it provided the single thread he needed. With John Breton dead and safely atomized, nobody in the world would believe the kind of story Kate would have to tell should she ever accuse him of murder. And, in time, he could allay any suspicions she might have. The pounding certainty in his destiny nurtured over nine agonized years, surged through him again, sweeping away all the doubts of the past few days. He had created the Time B universe, he had created Kate – and still held both in the palm of his hand. It was going to take a little longer than he had anticipated, that was all . . .

He raised his head from the struggle with Kate and glanced

around the bedroom. A closet door was open where she had been taking out clothes for her proposed trip to the lodge. He dragged Kate off the bed, pushed her into the closet and slid the doors together. As an afterthought, he took the spool of fishing line from his pocket and lapped it around the door handles, converting the closet to a miniature prison.

Breathing heavily, and dabbing the scratches on his face with his handkerchief, Breton ran downstairs and out to the car. He had one more task to perform that day.

The relatively simple one of projecting John Breton, not into Time A, but into eternity.

FIFTEEN

BLAIZE CONVERY CARRIED a tapering plastic cup of coffee to his desk and placed it carefully at the right-hand side.

He sat down on the creaking swing-chair and opened the desk's flat central drawer. From it he took his pipe, tobacco pouch, lighter, pipe tamper and a bundle of white woolly cleaners. These he arranged in an orderly square, formating with the vapouring coffee cup, with the air of a master craftsman setting out his tools. He then opened a deep drawer, took out a thick oatmeal-coloured file, and placed it in the centre of the little quadrangle he had so carefully prepared. With all the necessary formalities completed, he gave a deep sigh of contentment and began to leaf through the file.

It had been a dull, routine sort of a day – most of it spent doing legwork on a case which had been successfully prosecuted a month earlier, but which had involved a mammoth tangle of legal loose-ends. He had been in and out of his car fifty times in the pursuit of three unimportant signatures, his back hurt and his feet felt swollen inside his shoes. But this was his part of the day – the extra hour he often took when his shift had officially ended, the hour in which he was free to follow his instincts along any ghost-trail they could discern.

He sipped his coffee, filled and lit his pipe, and allowed their subtle influences to carry him into realms of concentration where the yellowed sheets and blurred carbon characters seemed to come to life and whisper the innermost thoughts of the men whose names they preserved. Within minutes, Convery was caught up in his own form of time travel, and the big, crowded office bleached away as he burrowed into the past, paring it gently, layer by layer . . .

'Come on, Blaize,' a voice boomed in his ear. 'Snap out of it, boy.'

Convery looked up, struggling to wrench his mind back into his body, and saw the sandy eyebrows and splay-toothed smile of Boyd Leyland, another lieutenant in the homicide division.

'Hi, Boyd.' Convery concealed his annoyance – Leyland was a good friend and an able cop. 'I didn't know you were on today.'

'I'm not!' Leyland always sounded triumphant. 'I got Saturdays off this month, but I wouldn't let the team down. Not me, boy, not me.'

Covery stared at him blankly for a second, then he remembered. This was October and the Saturday night bowling sessions were on again. 'Oh, we're bowling tonight.' He failed to sound enthusiastic.

'Of course we are. Let's go, boy!'

'Look Boyd, I don't think I can make it tonight.'

Leyland was instantly sympathetic. 'Are they working the ass off you, too? Last week I had to do three . . .' He broke off as his gaze took in the file opened in front of Convery. His jaw dropped and he beckoned excitedly to a group of men standing nearby.

'Hey, fellows – he's at it again! You know how old Professor Convery's spending his Saturday night? He's back on the Spiedel case!' Incredulity made Leyland's voice almost falsetto. 'He's back on the Goddam Spiedel case!'

'I'm too beat to bowl tonight,' Convery announced defensively. 'I just want to sit here.'

'Bull!' Leyland shot out his big red hands, closed the old

file and dragged Convery out of his chair. 'We need all the steady men we can get this year. The exercise'll do you good, anyway.'

'All right, all right.'

Convery saw he had no chance of winning. While the others waited, he regretfully tidied up his desk then joined them as they rolled down the corridor towards the elevator. The noisy delight his workmates were taking in the prospects of an evening of bowling and beer failed to communicate itself to him. *Yesterday he had talked to a guilty man.*

Convery was coldly certain of Breton's guilt, and he also now believed he would never be able to bring Breton to justice – but these were not the things which gnawed at his soul. It was the fact that he could not understand the nature of the crime.

Something very strange had happened in the Breton household nine years ago, and the effects of it were being felt to this day, flaring up to their own occult rhythm like the symptoms of an ineradicable disease. *But what had happened?* Convery had blunted his mental armoury on the problem, and he was left with a baffled yearning to penetrate that household, to live there, to grill and sift and analyse until he knew both its members better than they knew themselves . . .

'Come on, Blaize.' Leyland opened the door of his car. 'I'll give you a ride to the alley.'

Convery glanced around the police parking lot, suddenly aware of the old icy churning in his belly. 'No thanks. I'll take my own – I might have to leave early.'

'Hop in,' Leyland commanded. 'You won't be leaving early, boy.'

Convery shook his head. 'I might be leaving late, then. Go ahead – I'll see you there.'

Leyland shrugged and folded himself into his car. Convery found his Plymouth in the rapidly growing dusk and slid behind the wheel, with the siren-song loud in his ears. At the first intersection he swung away from behind Leyland's car and gunned the Plymouth across town, fleeing as though his friends would come after him. They would not do that, of course, but they would be hurt and caustic; just as Gina had been when he'd walked out of the kids' birthday party. But his demon was perched firmly on his shoulder, and his destiny was never to resist its blandishments.

Reaching the avenue in which the Bretons lived, Convery slowed down and drifted his care between the walls of trees with an almost silent engine. The big house was in complete darkness. Disappointment welled up in him as he brought the car to a halt. So the demon had deceived him, as had happened so many times in the past. Convery glanced at his watch and calculated he could reach the bowling alley in time to get away with a claim to have been filled up with gas. It was the sensible thing to do, and yet . . .

'Ah, hell!'

He exclaimed in disgust as he found himself getting out of the car to walk back to the house. Above him the darkening sky was teeming with meteorites, but they scarcely registered on his brain. The gravel of the drive crunched underfoot as he moved up the shadowed tunnel of shrubbery and along the side, past the porch.

He stepped on to the patio and surveyed the rear of the house. No lights there, either – which was what he had expected. The garage doors were open, showing that John Breton's Turbo-Lincoln was gone and that Mrs Breton's sports model was still there. Obviously, the Bretons had gone out together. Convery flicked his teeth with a thumbnail. He had a definite impression that the Bretons did not go around much together, but there was nothing to stop them spending an evening in each other's company if they wanted to try it out. There was certainly no law against it – which was not the case where snooping on private property was concerned.

Convery rocked on his heels, undecided, and was turning away when the kitchen door creaked faintly.

He went closer and saw it was ajar and moving slightly in the evening breeze. It swung wide open, emitting a billow of warm air, when he pushed it gingerly with his toe. At last provided with a vestige of a reason for being there, Convery went into the dark kitchen and put on the lights.

'Anybody there?' he shouted, feeling slightly self-conscious.

A frenzy of hammering broke out immediately in the upper part of the house, and he thought he could hear a woman's cries. Flicking lights on as he went, Convery ran up the stairs and followed the sound to a front bedroom. The hammering was coming from a closet. He tried to open it and discovered unbreakable fishing line lapped around the handles. The steel-hard knots flaked his fingernails away as he tried to open them. He stood back and kicked one of the handles completely off the door.

A fraction of a second later, Kate Breton was in his arms, and the arctic exultation was pouring through him as he realized the demon was going to be kind to him after all.

'Mrs Breton,' he said urgently. 'What's going on here? Who locked you in the closet?'

'Jack Breton,' she said. Her eyes were empty, drained.

'You mean your husband did this?'

'No – not my husband. It was ...' She stopped, drew a shuddering breath and he saw awareness flood back into her, subtly altering the lines of her face. Invisible barriers clanged into place between them.

'Tell me what happened, Mrs Breton.'

'You've got to help me, Lieutenant.' She was still afraid, but the period of mindless panic had passed. 'I think my husband has been kidnapped. He's at Lake Pasco. Will you drive me there? Will you drive me to Lake Pasco?'

'But ...'

'Have mercy on me, Lieutenant – I'm asking you for my *husband*!'

'Let's go,' he said grimly. An opportunity had passed, but he had a feeling that Lake Pasco was the place where he would finally learn to talk with his hands.

SIXTEEN

IN THE FIRST part of the journey to the lodge, Breton came near to death several times through trying to take corners in powered drifts which would have been beyond the design limits of a racing jet.

He was well clear of the city before he regained enough control of his right foot to let him lift it off the floor, and the big car slowed its nightmare rush through the darkness. To get killed in a car crash at this stage would be pathetic, he reminded himself, although it would have some interesting consequences. As soon as the activity of his central nervous system came to an end, the chronomotor module embedded in his left wrist would be robbed of its energy source – and his body would vanish back into Time A.

The situation could be even more intriguing if his death was not instantaneous, but occurred in an ambulance rushing him to a hospital. How, he wondered, would the ambulance team even begin to explain the disappearance of one full-size John Doe?

The mental game calmed Breton's nerves sufficiently to let him think constructively about what had to be done within the next hour. In outline, the schedule of events was simple – kill John Breton, transport his body to the large-bore drilling site, and get rid of it. But there could be practical difficulties. Suppose, for instance, that the drilling operation was running behind its timetable and there was a crew working around the clock? . . .

Relieved at finding himself a rational being again, Breton began looking for the side road where he had earlier noticed the construction company's sign. As soon as he began to pay attention to it the road started to seem unfamiliar. He slowed the car even further and scanned the east side of the road, hesitating at every winding side track, until he saw the looming grey-white square of the sign. His headlights picked out the name of the Breton Consultancy in one of the panels allocated to the sub-contractors, and he swung the car off the highway. It waltzed gently along the deep ruts made by heavy construction vehicles, sending dust clouds curling away on each side.

Less than five minutes from the highway the side road petered out into a flat, chewed-up area where earth-moving equipment had been at work. Breton zigzagged the car, its headlights searching through ranges of building materials, until he saw the familiar turret-shaped structures of the boring rigs. There was nobody near them or anywhere else on the machine-scarred site. He wheeled around and drove back to the highway, contented with his return on the few minutes the detour had taken.

As he drove north, he felt his confidence grow stronger. For a time it had seemed as though things were going wrong, as though the Time B world was going to betray its creator, but it had been his own fault. Somehow the days John, Kate and he had spent together had robbed him of his former strength and certainty . . .

The night sky ahead of the car was suddenly lit up with a pulsing brilliance.

A miniature sun raced across his vision on a descending curve, huge writhing blankets of flame breaking away behind it as it vanished behind a tree-clad ridge less than a mile away. The trees were outlined in the rayed light of an explosion, and then the awful sound of it engulfed the car, paralysing Breton with primeval fears. A series of diminishing thunderclaps followed the original explosion, dying away into Olympian grumbles and growls, in the air all around.

Breton found himself drenched with sweat, hurtling on through the night in unearthly silence. Several seconds pounded by before his power of reason re-emerged timidly from its cave into the twentieth century and told him he had witnessed a meteorite impact. He swore feebly under his breath and tightened his grip on the steering wheel.

The sky, he thought with abrupt, baffled conviction, *is my enemy.*

He reached the crest of the ridge and far away to his left saw topaz fragments of flame stirring on the sloping grasslands.

Within a matter of minutes the whole area would be overrun with curious sightseers. Breton knew the mentality of the average Montana city-dweller – even a simple brushfire was enough to bring them pouring out of their desiccated houses, ridiculously grateful at having somewhere to go in their brand-new cars, which – big and fast though they were – were unable to perform their function as magic carpets in the face of the prairie vastness.

An event like a meteor strike would draw them in from a hundred miles, and even further when the local radio stations got hold of the news. It meant that on the return journey along this same road, with a dead man in the trunk, he would probably be working his way through heavy traffic. There was a strong possibility that the police would have had to set up traffic control points. Breton got a vision of hard-faced, blue-uniformed men slapping the trunk as he crawled by, just as Lieutenant Convery had done the day before.

The prospect alarmed him, yet – in a way – the meteorite had done him a favour. There would be little likelihood of anybody taking note of, or remembering, the movements of one car. He increased speed slightly to get clear of the area before the traffic began to pile up.

The lodge would have been in darkness when he arrived had it not been for the uneasily shifting brilliance of the aurora in the north, and the manic tracer-fire of meteors carving the night sky into diamond-shaped fragments. Breton got out of the car and walked quickly towards the lodge, pressing one hand on the outside of his jacket pocket to prevent the pistol from jarring against his hip.

In the variable, unnatural light the solid lines of the fishing lodge seemed to shrink, quiver and expand in a kind of plasmatic glee. Once more Breton felt cold and desperately tired. He opened the front door and went into the sentient darkness, some instinct making him take the pistol out of his pocket. At the head of the basement stairs he hesitated before turning on the light.

The blinking, then steadying, glow of the fluorescents revealed John Breton lying on his side in the centre of the floor. His stained and dusty clothing gave him the appearance of a dead creature, but his eyes were intelligent, watchful.

'I tried to get away,' he said, almost casually, as Jack went down the stairs. 'Nearly cut my hands off.'

He moved as if to try to exhibit his wrists, then his eyes took in the pistol in Jack's hand.

'Already?' His voice was sad rather than afraid.

Jack realized he had been half-hiding the weapon behind his body. Reluctantly, he brought it into full view.

'Are you going to stand up?'

'There hardly seems much point.' John seemed aware that he had some obscure psychological advantage. 'What would it achieve?'

'All right.' Jack released the safety catch on the pistol and aimed it. There was nothing to be gained by wasting time. Nothing in the world.

'Ah, no.' John's voice was beginning to quaver. 'You're really going to do it, aren't you?'

'I have to. I'm sorry.'

'I'm sorry, too – for us all.'

'Save the piety for yourself.'

Jack tightened his finger on the trigger, but it seemed to have acquired the stiffness of a hydraulic ram, and the seconds dragged by. John lay still for a moment, then his resolve broke and he began to squirm frantically, trying to put distance between himself and the gun muzzle. His feet scrabbled on the concrete as he worked to back away. Jack braced his gun arm with his left hand, and went after him doggedly. At last the trigger began its stealthy, pre-orgasmic slide.

Suddenly, cool air gusted past Jack Breton.

He turned, almost firing the pistol in panic. A ghostly, transparent object hung in the air a few feet away. Breton's face contorted with shock as he identified the familiar, terrible, bilobular shape.

A human brain!

As he watched, a corded vertical column materialized beneath the insubstantial brain, followed by cloudy, branching networks of finer lines, until – within the space of a second – it resembled a three-dimensional plastic model of the human nervous system.

There was a further, stronger, gust of cool air. And Jack Breton found himself staring, paralysed, into the face of another man.

I too must have looked like that, Jack Breton thought, in the first tortured instant. I must have looked like that – once – when I kept that rendezvous by the three trees . . . a naked brain, materializing there in the darkness, awful, pulsating, loathsome. With the spreading nervous networks reaching downwards, like a racing fungus, until they were clothed by my own flesh. It was one aspect of chronomotion he had never considered – the arrival and its . . .

The detailed, convergent thought was blotted out by a sudden, jolting awareness of its significance.

'Put the gun away, Jack.'

The stranger spoke in a lifeless monotone which nonetheless conveyed a sense of crushing urgency. He moved closer to Jack Breton, and the overhead tube bathed his face in cold light. Breton's first impression was that Nature had made a hideous mistake in fashioning this face – it seemed to have only one eye, and two mouths!

As he brought it into visual and intellectual focus, he saw that the face had indeed only one eye. The missing orb had been completely excised allowing the whole region of the socket to collapse inwards, and no attempt had been made to disguise or cover the loss. The upper and lower lids met each other in a perfect, sardonic little smile, startlingly similar to the one which twisted the stranger's lips.

Breton received an impression of greying hair that failed to cover patches of diseased scalp, of heavily lined skin, of shabby, strangely-styled clothes – but all his attention was riveted on that ghastly second mouth.

'Who . . .?' he forced the words out. 'Who are you?'

The answer came not from the stranger, but from the floor.

'Don't you recognize him, Jack?' John Breton spoke with a kind of detached reproach. 'That's yourself.'

'No!' Jack Breton stepped back, instinctively raising the pistol. 'It isn't true.'

'But he *is*.' John sounded revengeful. 'This is the one aspect of this whole time travel business in which I've got more experience than you, Jack. You never gave me credit for recognizing and accepting you so quickly that first night . . .'

'Don't argue!' The stranger interrupted tiredly but authoritatively, like a dying emperor. 'I hadn't realized the two of you would be so like children – and there's so little time.'

John Breton struggled to his feet. 'Are you going to untie me?'

'There isn't time,' the stranger said, shaking his head. 'I will use no violence, and will do nothing which might precipitate violence. I can use only . . . words.'

'I asked who you are,' Jack Breton said.

'You know who I am.' The stranger sounded even more tired, as though his strength was failing. 'When you were planning to cross into this time-stream you labelled yourself Breton A, and John here as Breton B. I have reason to dislike those unemotional tags – so I'll accept the name of Breton Senior. It is much more appropriate.'

'I could put a bullet through you,' Breton pointed out, almost irrelevantly, in an attempt to subdue the dismay he could feel building up inside him.

'Why bother? You've made one trip back through time yourself, and have a good idea of what it does to the nervous system. You must know I can sustain this strain only for a very short period, and then I'll be sucked back to fill the temporal vacuum I've created in my own time.'

Breton nodded, remembering the way he had lain pole-axed in the grass after he had shot Spiedel. And that jump had lasted only a few seconds. He tried to visualize what Breton Senior would go through on his return, but his mind was already a whirling storm of half-formulated questions . . .

'You were able to make that jump because, combined with your unusual cerebral structure, you had an overpowering need to go back and correct a mistake. But your obsession led you into a vastly greater mistake. A mistake which has two entirely different aspects – one of them personal, one of them universal.' The older man's voice wavered slightly. He walked to the cluttered workbench and leaned against it. The stiffness of his movements reminded Jack Breton of how difficult it had been to walk with the network of wires taped to his skin.

'The personal mistake,' Breton Senior continued, 'was in not learning to live with the tragedy of Kate's death, and living with it includes accepting your share of the responsibility. Tragedies happen to many people, but the measure of their worth in human beings lies in their ability to surmount tragedy and find new meaning for their lives.

'Does this sound like *Reader's Digest* stuff to you?'

Jack Breton nodded.

'I thought it might, but even you – although you can't admit it – have begun to realize the truth of what I've been saying. Where *is* the happiness you thought the Time B world held for you, Jack? Has it all worked out the way you expected?'

Breton hesitated only momentarily, glancing across at John Breton. 'It's working out. I have a problem with Kate, but that's a personal matter . . .'

'Wrong!' Breton Senior's single eye gleamed like a beacon. 'There's another reason you must return to your own probability world. If you don't it means – quite simply that you will have destroyed two universes!'

The words had a strangely familiar ring to Jack Breton, as though he had heard them long ago, in a forgotten dream. His first instinct was to scream a denial, but some part of his mind had known for a long time . . . that the sky was his enemy. He felt his knees begin to swim.

'Go on,' he said faintly.

'On what level do you want it?'

'The most basic.'

'All right. As you'll remember from your intensive study of electrical phenomena, you decided that the basic problem in building a chronomotive device was the abrogation of Kirchoff's laws. You had a special interest in the second law and the fact that the algebraic sum of the electromotive forces in any closed circuit or mesh is equal to the algebraic sum of the products of the resistance of each portion of—'

'You'll have to make it more basic,' Jack Breton interrupted. 'I can't *think*.'

'Very well – my time's running out, anyway. We'll move on to the law of conservation of energy and mass. The universe is an absolutely closed system, and has to obey the principle that the sum of its mass and energy must remain constant. Until you left the Time A universe it contained all the mass and energy that it had ever possessed or ever would possess.' Breton Senior had begun to speak more quickly.

'But you, Jack, are a creature of mass and energy, and in leaving the Time A universe you created a loss where no loss could possibly be sustained. And in entering the Time B universe you created a gain, an overload on the space-time fabric. Imbalances like that can be maintained only for brief periods ...'

'So *that*'s it,' John Breton said softly, coming into the conversation for the first time. 'That's what's been going on – the changes in the gravitic constant, the meteors, all the rest of it.' He stared at Jack in startled speculation. 'It *did* start that night you showed up. I remember it now. I even saw a couple of meteors when Gordon and Miriam were driving off. And that was the night Carl called up and said—'

'My time here is almost finished,' Breton Senior cut in. He had slumped sideways on the bench and his voice had shrunk to an agonized whisper. 'Jack, the longer you remain outside your own universe, the more certainly you will set up the growing imbalances which will destroy both time-streams. You must return – *now*.'

'I still don't understand this.' Jack Breton took a deep breath and tried forcing his brain into action. 'You say that by remaining here I'll destroy the universe, yet you, apparently, have come back to this point in time – from the future you say doesn't exist.'

'How big of a jump do you think I made?'

'I don't know.' Jack Breton began to feel afraid.

'Twenty years? Thirty years?' Breton Senior pressed.

'Something like that.'

'It was just over four years.'

'But . . .' Jack was aghast, and he noticed the shock register on John's face too.

'I'm four years older than you are.' Breton Senior made an obvious effort to rally his strength. 'But I see that you still haven't grasped the situation fully. It's my fault for not making it clearer, but I assumed you would understand . . .

'Don't you see, Jack? I am what you will become if you murder your Time B self and live on in this time-stream with Kate. I went through with it, just as you were about to do when I got here, and I got away with it.

'Got away with it!' Breton Senior laughed, in a way that Jack Breton had never heard anyone laugh before, then he went on speaking – but not to either of the men present – his broken phrases sketching in the lineaments of the face of Armageddon.

As the bonds of gravity were slackened the planets stole away from their parent sun, seeking new orbits commensurate with the altered balance of gravitic and radial forces. But they did not move quickly enough, for the Sun came after them like a demented mother intent on the slaughter of her own children. Bloated, swelling with the nuclear pus of her own dissolution, she bombarded her offspring with unimaginable quantitites of lethal radiation.

Breton Senior existed four years in a world which had become an arena for two different forms of death, each struggling for the maximum share of humanity's carcass. The ancient decimators of famine and plague warred with new competitiors – epidemic cancer and epidemic non-viable mutation.

When Kate succumbed to a nameless disease, he dis-

covered within himself something which had been absent since his first trip back through time – the chronomotive potential, which in others was known as remorse. He began to build a new chronomotor and, even though hampered by the loss of a diseased eye, finished it in a matter of weeks. His intention was to persuade Breton A to go back into his own time-stream, thus restoring universal balance before it was too late.

If he was successful, the B time-stream leading to the death of the universe would still continue on its accelerating downwards course – nothing could be done about that – but it would also produce an offshoot stream. This would be a modified Time B probability world in which Kate and John Breton could live out their lives in peace.

The rewards, as far as Breton Senior was concerned, would be philosophical rather than practical – for the cold equations of chronomotive physics dictated that if he tried to enjoy that world his presence there would destroy it. But, having seen what he had seen, he was prepared to settle for the knowledge that the other world existed, somewhere, somewhen.

At first, when arranging the jump, he planned to take a rifle and make sure that Jack Breton returned to his own universe – just as, in that remote earlier life, he had ejected Spiedel from the land of the living.

But that would have been the easy way, and he had done with killing.

If he could not influence Jack Breton by reason alone, then he would die with the awful burden of knowing that he had taken every other living creature in the universe with him . . .

As he listened, Jack Breton felt the insupportable weight of two universes transferred to his own shoulders. His grotesque older self's descriptions of the agony and horror that lay in this time-stream's future struck deeply into Jack's soul and body; he felt a wrenching sickness growing in his stomach, chilling sweat covering him. His own private universe was crumbling about him, and he wanted to deny it, to shout '*No!*' as though that would change things.

But Breton Senior stood waiting before him, a Dorian Gray image of his past and his future.

Shuddering, he threw the pistol aside and ran forward, grasping Breton Senior's hand.

'All right – I'll go back,' he whispered. 'You can let go now. I promise.'

Breton Senior hesitated, judging; but then, perhaps realizing he had no more time, he said:

'Thanks.'

The vibrations of the single word were still in the air when Breton Senior had vanished. Jack Breton found himself staring at the workbench through empty space. He turned helplessly and looked at John Breton, whose face had become ashen with shock. They experienced a moment of pure understanding which had nothing to with telepathy.

'I ...' Jack searched for words. 'I'll get you out of that fishing line.'

'I'd appreciate it. I'll still hate your guts, though.'

'Can't say I blame you.'

Breton opened the workbench drawer and found another spool of fishing line. He took it to the centre of the basement and used its pressure guillotine to cut the line around John's wrists. It parted with a metallic click. He was fitting the jaws of the guillotine over the line connecting John's arm to the ceiling joist when he heard a car slither to a halt outside. The sound was followed by the banging of two doors.

Jack Breton shoved the spool into John's blood-streaked hand and ran to the workbench. He leaped on to it and pulled aside the curtains of the window above. In the garish light from the heavens he saw the outline of Convery's Plymouth. Kate was already running towards the lodge, the upper surfaces of her body limned in frosty silver. Breton filled his eyes for the last time. The sight of her oval face, long thighs, breasts uplifted by flight, sent pain flooding through him.

He let the curtain fall back in place and jumped down off the bench. In the tool drawer he found a small screwdriver.

He pushed his watch further up on his arm, positioned the screwdriver blade directly over the flat lump of the chrono-motor module, and hesitated, looking up at John.

'You want to say goodbye?'

'Goodbye.'

'Thanks.'

Jack Breton stabbed the narrow blade deep into his wrist, and the Time B world tilted ponderously away.

SEVENTEEN

CONVERY GOT OUT of the car more slowly than did Kate Breton.

There was no need to hurry at this stage. The answers he had been seeking for nine years were just a few yards from him, and there was no way they could escape him now. He wanted to move gently, with the windows of his mind wide open, drinking it all in – because this was fulfilment.

The shifting light from the sky was bright enough to show each individual pebble. He noted the Turbo-Lincoln parked close to the boathouse, and was turning towards the lodge when he saw a shoe lying at the water's edge and picked it up. It was the black slip-on he had noticed in Breton's hand on the previous day. But why was it lying out here? Convery shrugged. Another piece that would have to be fitted into the puzzle when the final reckoning came.

Keeping the shoe in his hand, he jog-trotted towards the lodge behind Kate Breton. He had taken only a few paces when someone drew aside the curtain of a basement window at the front of the lodge, spilling white fluorescent light on the ground. A man's face appeared at the window. It could have been John Breton, but Convery was not sure. There might have been another man standing behind the one at the window, but at that instant a particularly bright spray of meteors raced across the sky, and their reflections on the glass turned it to beaten silver. The curtain fell back into place again.

Convery saw Kate Breton disappear into the lodge. He ran up the steps and into the central room. It was in darkness and he had to halt and grope for the light switch. When the lights came on he sprinted to the basement door, dragged it open and skidded to a standstill on the small wooden landing.

John and Kate Breton were standing in the centre of the basement. They were clinging to each other, and there was no other person present. Convery began to feel a premonition, the first stirrings of dismay.

'All right,' he snapped. 'Where is he?'

'Who?' John Breton looked up blankly.

'The guy who brought you here. The kidnapper.'

'Kidnapper?'

'Look – no games, please.' Convery went the rest of the way down the steps. 'Is there another way out of this building?'

'No.'

'Then where's the man who locked your wife in a closet and brought you here?'

'I'm sorry, Lieutenant,' Kate Breton said, raising her head from her husband's chest. 'It's all been a mistake. This is a ... domestic affair.'

'I'm not accepting that for an answer.' Convery kept his voice flat with an effort.

'But what other answer is there?'

'That's what I intend to find out. Have you looked at yourself in a mirror, John? You're in a mess – why's that?'

Breton shrugged. 'On weekends I'm a slob. Especially up here at the lake.'

'There's a piece of fishing line tied around your arm – why's that?'

'It just happened. I was measuring out some line and I tied myself in knots.'

Convery looked closely at Breton. His face was covered with day-old bruises, but it seemed to have acquired a strength which had never been there before. And there was the way the two Bretons were standing together, almost merged into one.

In the nature of Convery's job, he was not called upon to witness demonstrations of love very often – but he knew it when he saw it. That, too, was something that had been changed by the events of the last few days. Another part of the mystery.

'I've given you a lot of trouble for nothing,' Kate Breton said. 'Will you stay and have a drink with us?'

Convery shook his head, tasting defeat. 'I can see you two want to be alone.' Aware that his irony had been wasted, he turned to leave and remembered the shoe still in his hand. He held it out.

'Here's your shoe, John. I picked it up close to the water. I suppose you'd noticed you're going around with only one on?'

'Yes.' John Breton was grinning apologetically. 'When I decide to act like a slob, I really act like a slob.'

'That's what I thought you'd say. Goodnight!'

Convery went up the wooden steps tiredly, and out into the cool night air, his brow furrowed as he tried to assimilate the wealth of new clues he had received. Overhead, the meteor showers were still burning their way across the dark bowl of the sky, but they scarcely registered on his consciousness.

They were classified, in the filing system of his mind, as: 'Not relevant to the problem.'

Convery walked slowly to his car. And as he walked his right hand, of its own accord, began flexing, twisting and unflexing – waiting for the magical voice which would never come.

EIGHTEEN

TO JACK BRETON it seemed that someone had merely turned out the basement lights.

He stood in the sudden darkness, gasping with the intensity of the pain in his wrist, and listening intently for any sound of movement upstairs. After a few seconds he relaxed. The lodge was cold and empty in the Time A universe, and not owned by a Breton. Suppose, the thought came, it isn't owned by anybody, that the basement is locked up tight from the outside?

Breton took a step forward and, on the instant of moving off balance, felt his legs buckle beneath him. He fell forward helplessly, thudded against what felt like a large packing case, and sprawled on the dusty floor. When he tried to scramble to his feet, his arms and legs trembled violently and gave way, throwing him back down on his face.

The second time he was more cautious, gripping the packing case with both hands and working himself upward inch by inch. On his feet again, he leaned against the rough wood, breathing heavily.

Kate!

He stared around him blindly, chokingly aware that she was probably right there in the basement, separated from him only by the intangible barriers of probability. John Breton would be there, too, and their arms would be around each other.

Jack Breton tensed himself, waiting for the influx of pain; but – miraculously – none came. Instead, he felt the clean, pure taste of reconciliation. He had made a mistake once, but had corrected it. In the end he had put everything right again.

He groped his way towards the stairs and, moving slowly like an old man, reached the top. The door opened when he tried the handle. Beyond it the lodge's central room was lit by the garish, variable light sweeping in through the windows. The Time A world was experiencing its meteor showers too, but now that he had balanced the cosmic books everything would fall back into place again.

Before he closed the door behind him, Breton turned and stared down into the silent darkness of the empty basement.

'Excuse me,' he said, feeling foolish, but unable to prevent his lips from forming the words. 'I can see you two want to be alone.'

He had an illogical conviction they would get his message.